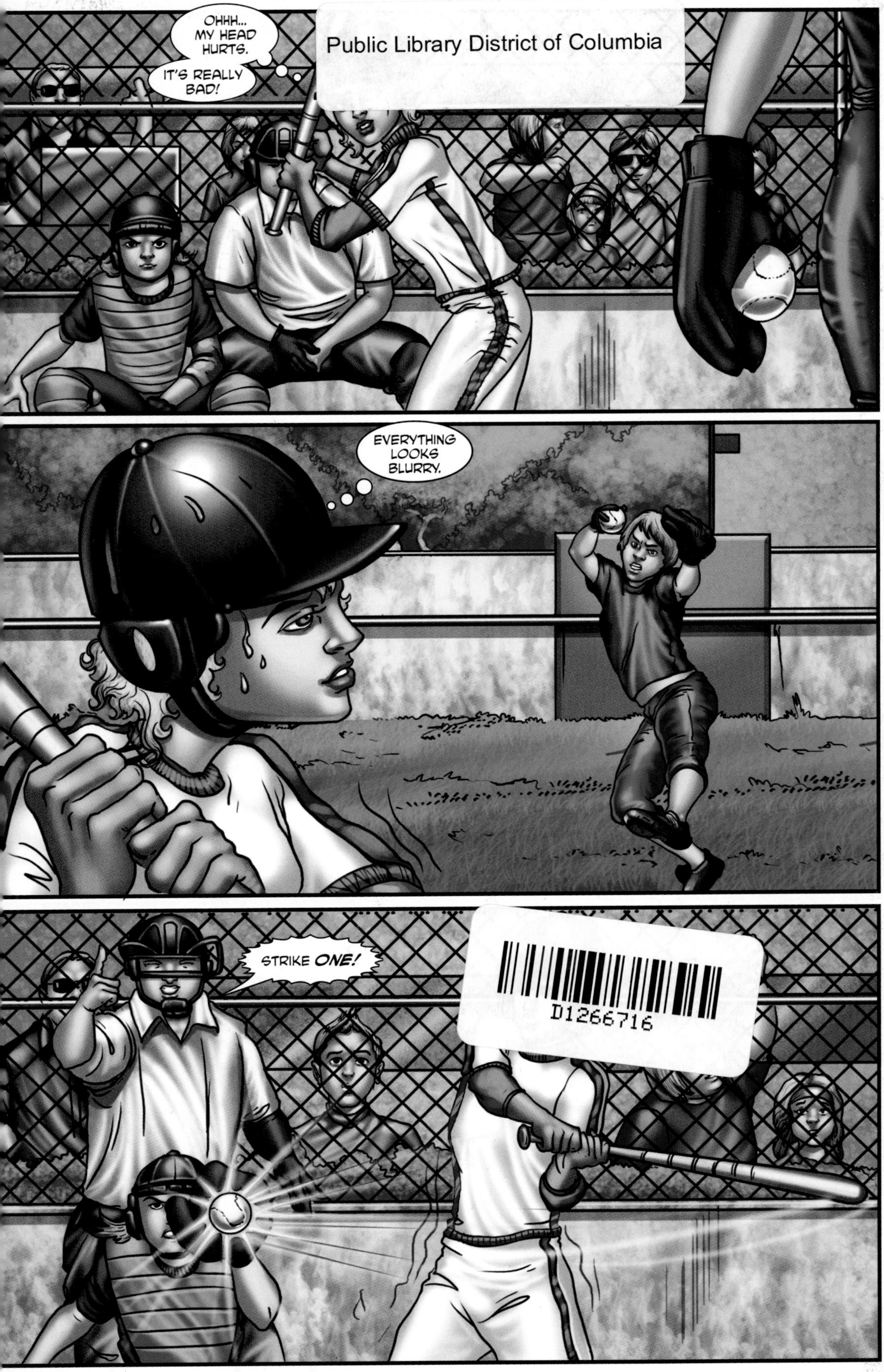
OHHH... MY HEAD HURTS.
IT'S REALLY BAD!
EVERYTHING LOOKS BLURRY.
STRIKE ONE!

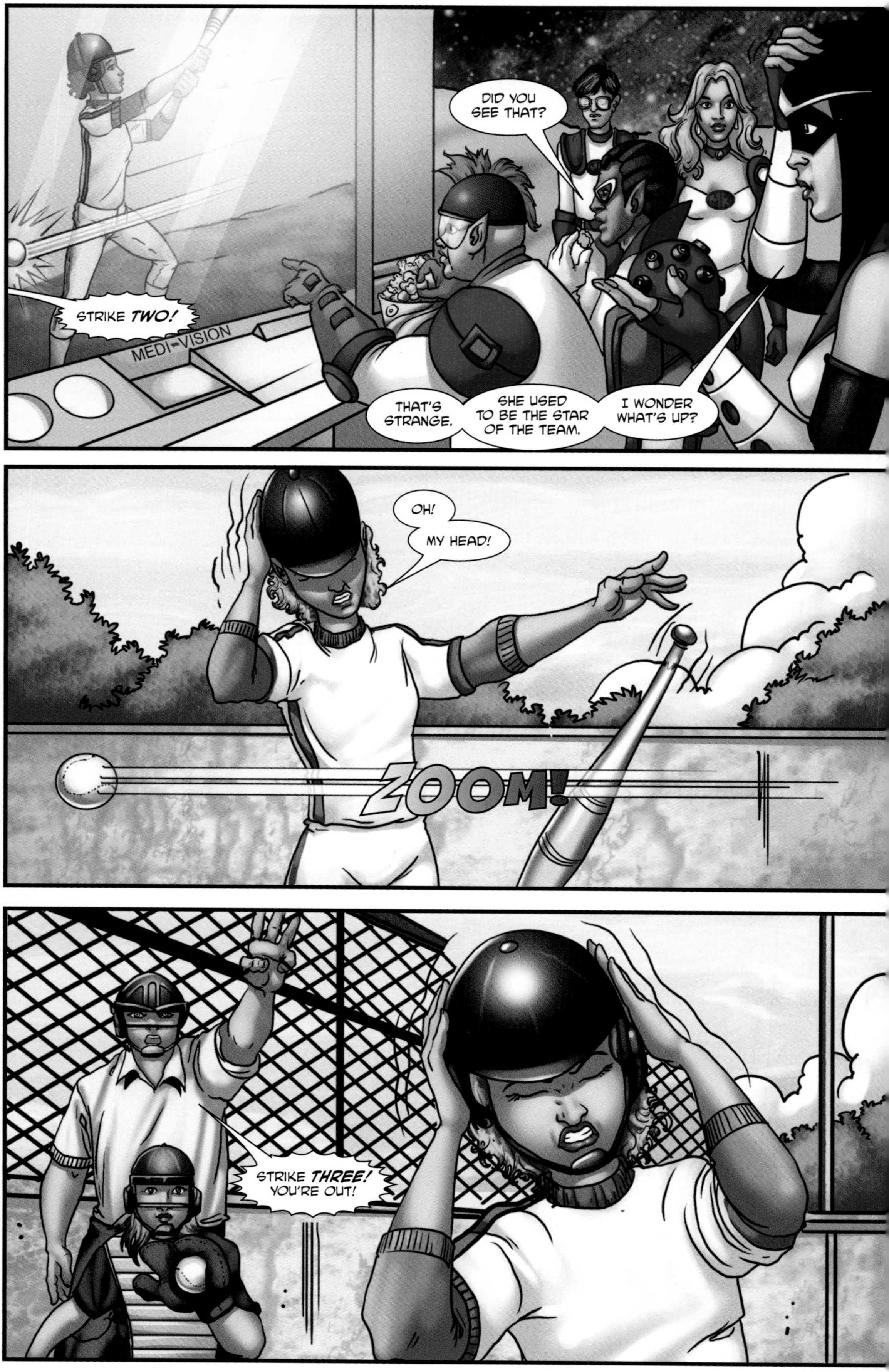
STRIKE TWO!
MEDI-VISION
DID YOU SEE THAT?
THAT'S STRANGE.
SHE USED TO BE THE STAR OF THE TEAM.
I WONDER WHAT'S UP?
OH!
MY HEAD!
ZOOM!
STRIKE THREE! YOU'RE OUT!

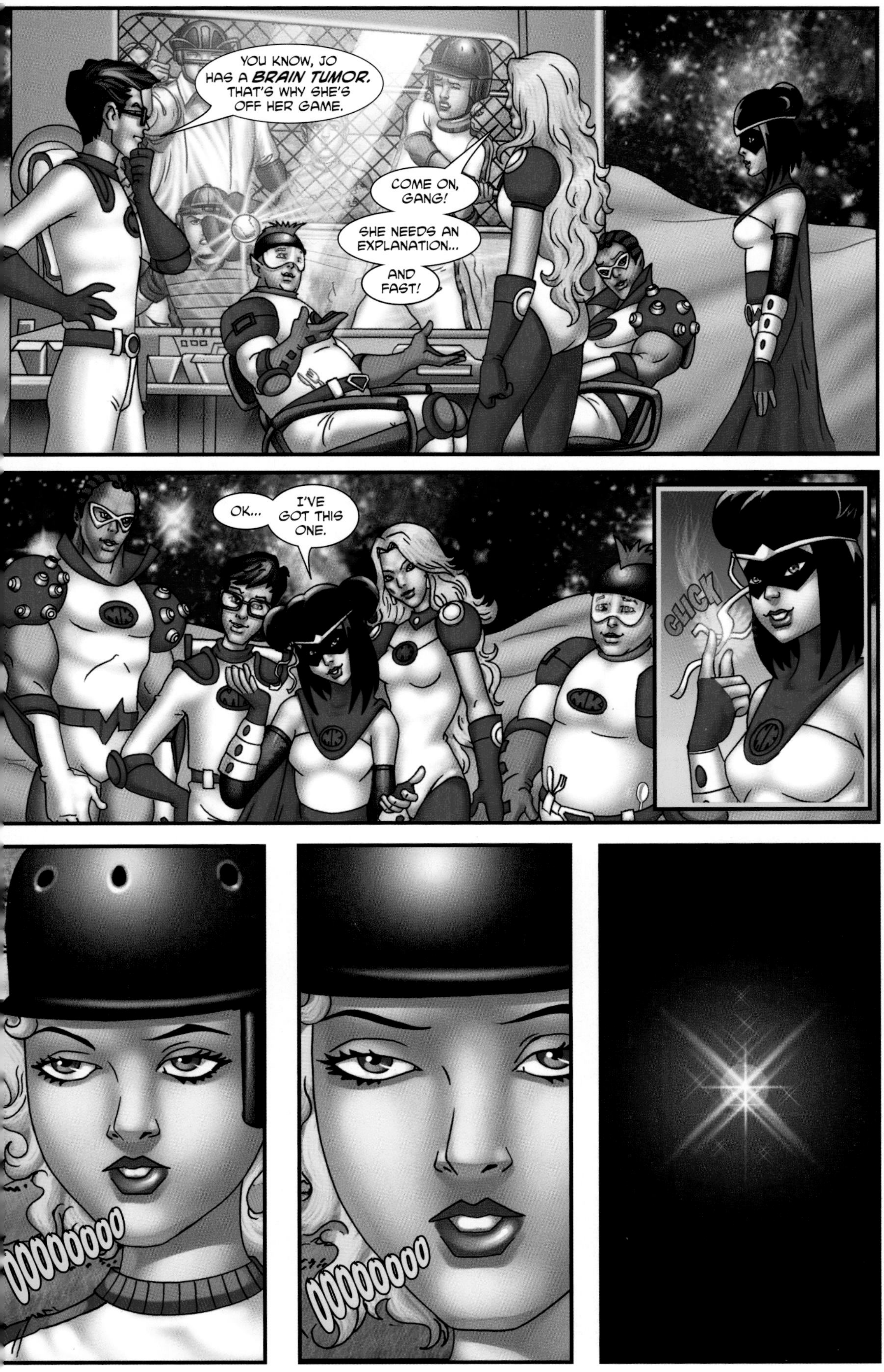

YOU KNOW, JO HAS A BRAIN TUMOR. THAT'S WHY SHE'S OFF HER GAME.
COME ON, GANG!
SHE NEEDS AN EXPLANATION...
AND FAST!
OK...
I'VE GOT THIS ONE.
CLICK
OOOOOOOO
OOOOOOOO

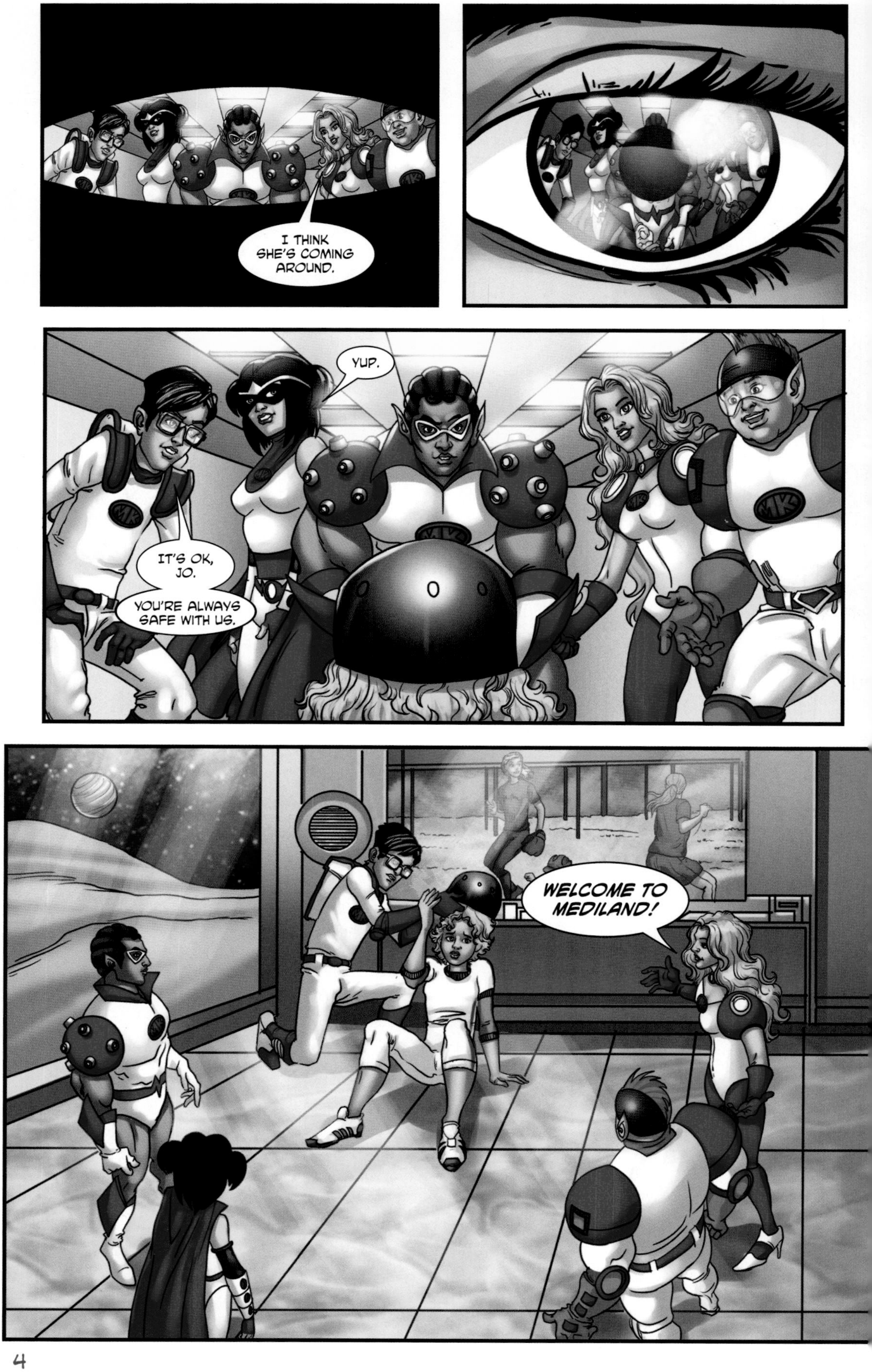
I THINK SHE'S COMING AROUND.
YUP.
IT'S OK, JO.
YOU'RE ALWAYS SAFE WITH US.
WELCOME TO MEDILAND!

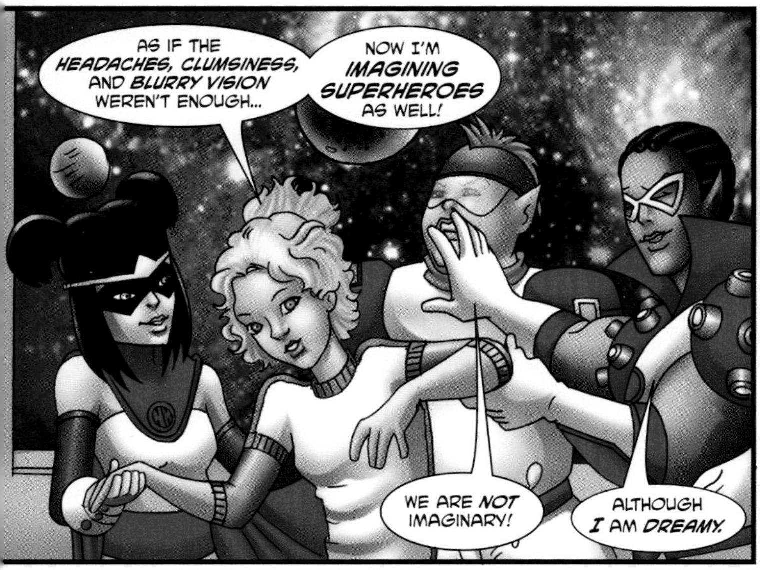
AS IF THE HEADACHES, CLUMSINESS, AND BLURRY VISION WEREN'T ENOUGH...
NOW I'M IMAGINING SUPERHEROES AS WELL!
WE ARE NOT IMAGINARY!
ALTHOUGH I AM DREAMY.

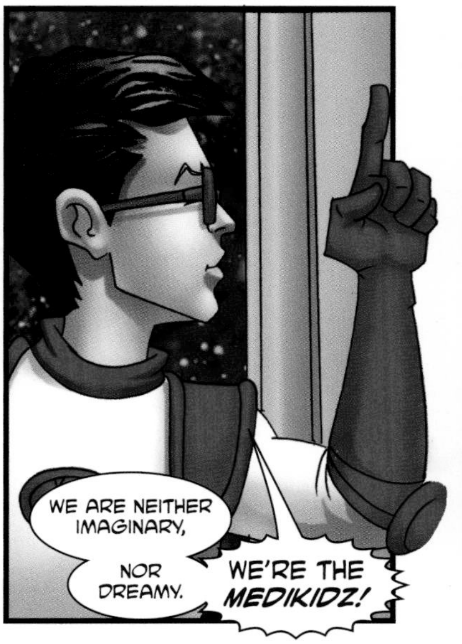
WE ARE NEITHER IMAGINARY,
NOR DREAMY.
WE'RE THE MEDIKIDZ!

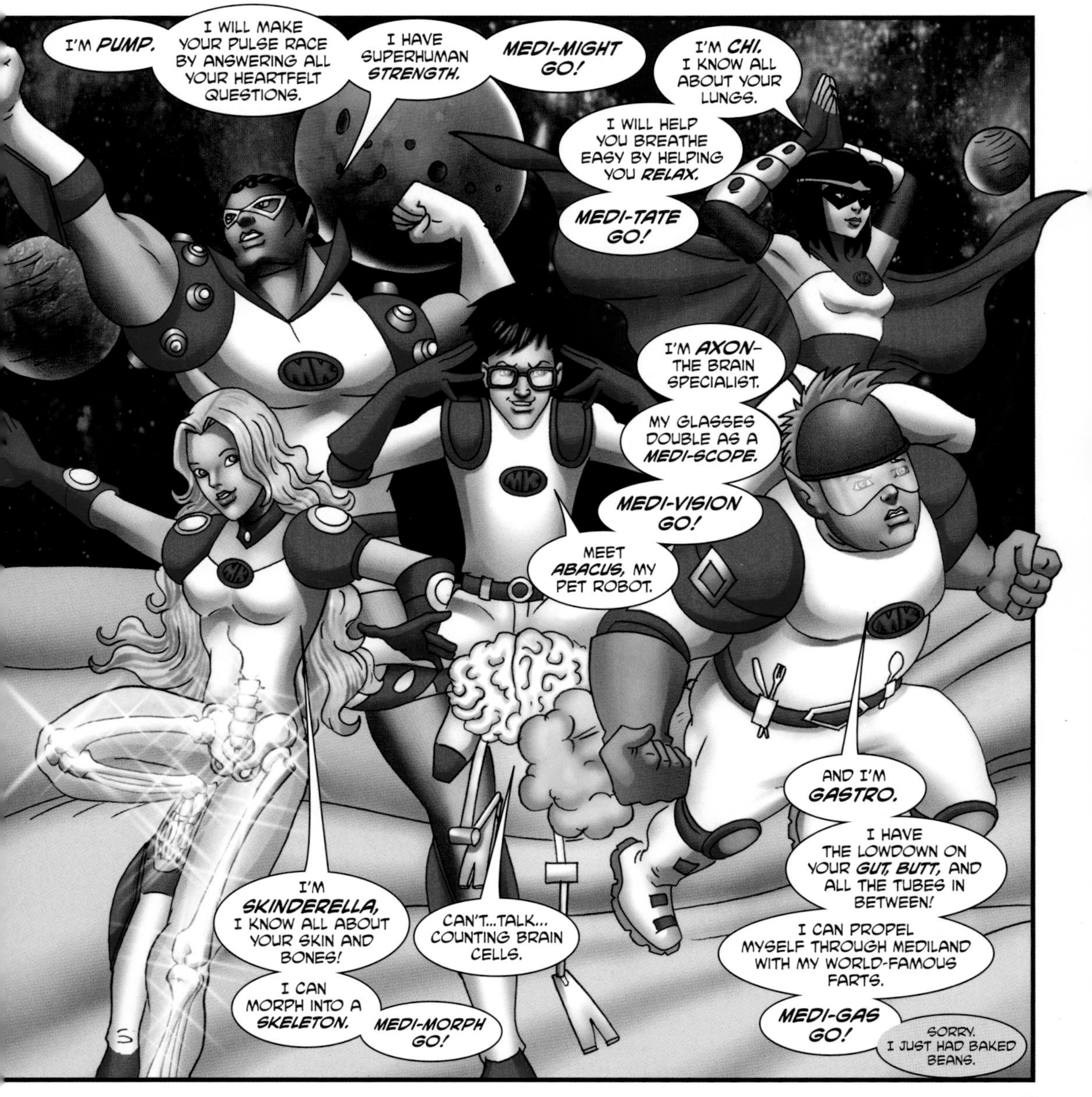
I'M PUMP.
I WILL MAKE YOUR PULSE RACE BY ANSWERING ALL YOUR HEARTFELT QUESTIONS.
I HAVE SUPERHUMAN STRENGTH.
MEDI-MIGHT GO!
I'M CHI. I KNOW ALL ABOUT YOUR LUNGS.
I WILL HELP YOU BREATHE EASY BY HELPING YOU RELAX.
MEDI-TATE GO!
I'M AXON- THE BRAIN SPECIALIST.
MY GLASSES DOUBLE AS A MEDI-SCOPE.
MEDI-VISION GO!
MEET ABACUS, MY PET ROBOT.
CAN'T...TALK... COUNTING BRAIN CELLS.
I'M SKINDERELLA, I KNOW ALL ABOUT YOUR SKIN AND BONES!
I CAN MORPH INTO A SKELETON.
MEDI-MORPH GO!
AND I'M GASTRO.
I HAVE THE LOWDOWN ON YOUR GUT, BUTT, AND ALL THE TUBES IN BETWEEN!
I CAN PROPEL MYSELF THROUGH MEDILAND WITH MY WORLD-FAMOUS FARTS.
MEDI-GAS GO!
SORRY. I JUST HAD BAKED BEANS.

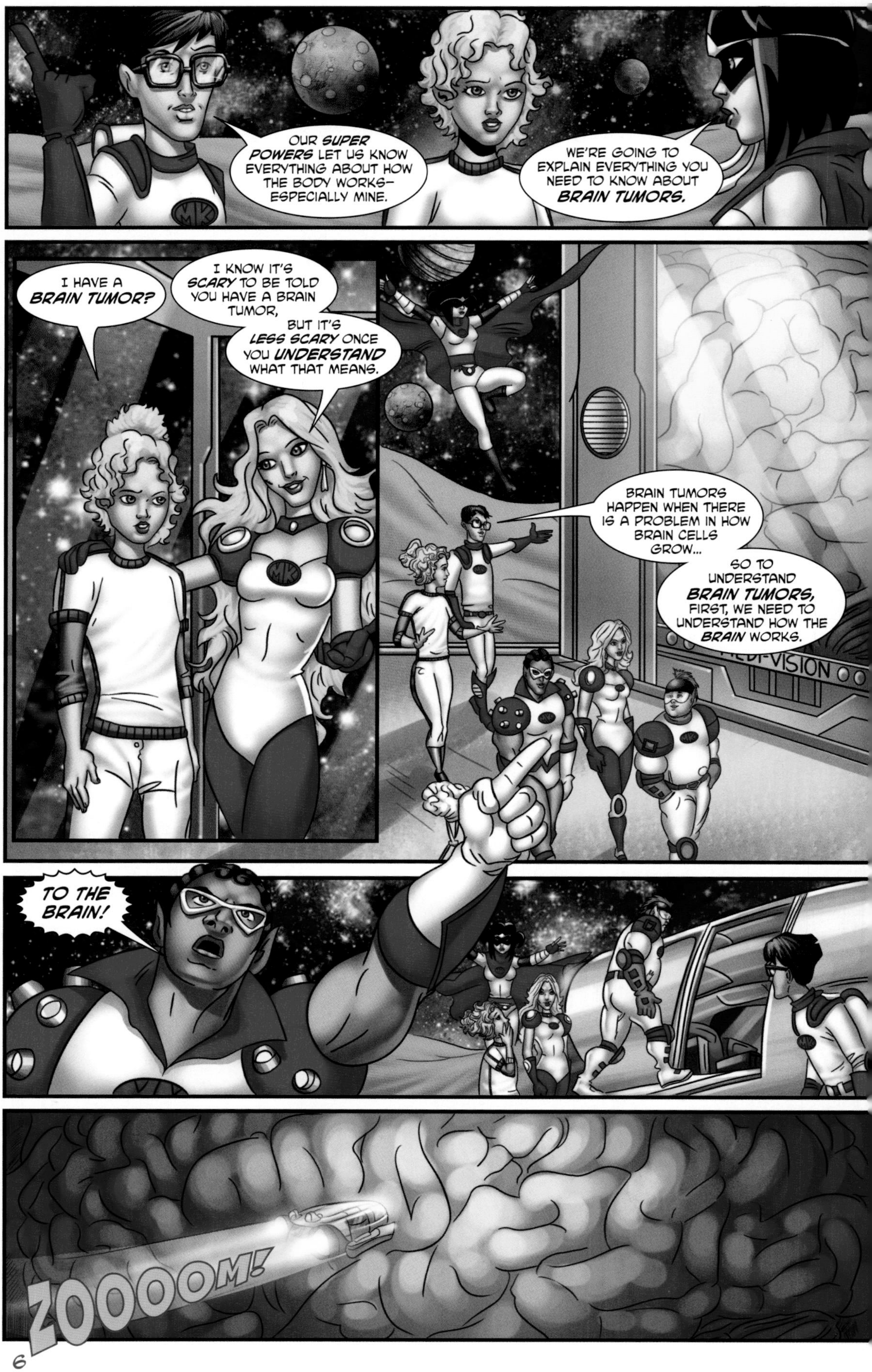
OUR SUPER POWERS LET US KNOW EVERYTHING ABOUT HOW THE BODY WORKS— ESPECIALLY MINE.
WE'RE GOING TO EXPLAIN EVERYTHING YOU NEED TO KNOW ABOUT BRAIN TUMORS.
I HAVE A BRAIN TUMOR?
I KNOW IT'S SCARY TO BE TOLD YOU HAVE A BRAIN TUMOR,
BUT IT'S LESS SCARY ONCE YOU UNDERSTAND WHAT THAT MEANS.
BRAIN TUMORS HAPPEN WHEN THERE IS A PROBLEM IN HOW BRAIN CELLS GROW...
SO TO UNDERSTAND BRAIN TUMORS, FIRST, WE NEED TO UNDERSTAND HOW THE BRAIN WORKS.
TO THE BRAIN!
ZOOOOM!

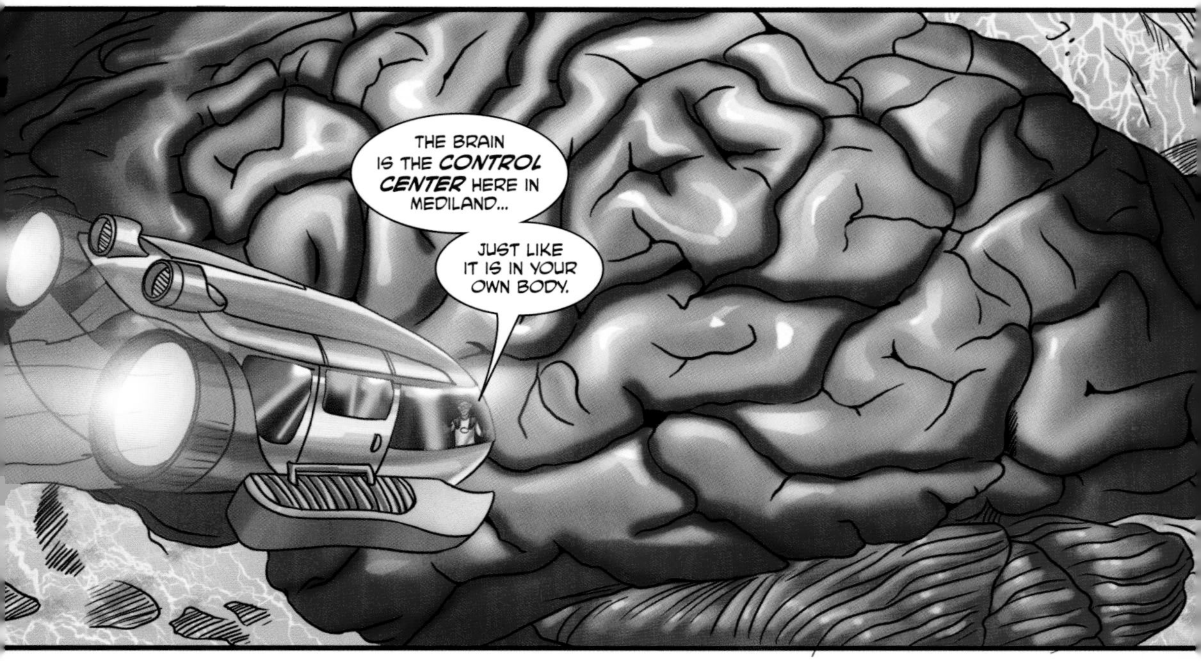
THE BRAIN IS THE CONTROL CENTER HERE IN MEDILAND...
JUST LIKE IT IS IN YOUR OWN BODY.

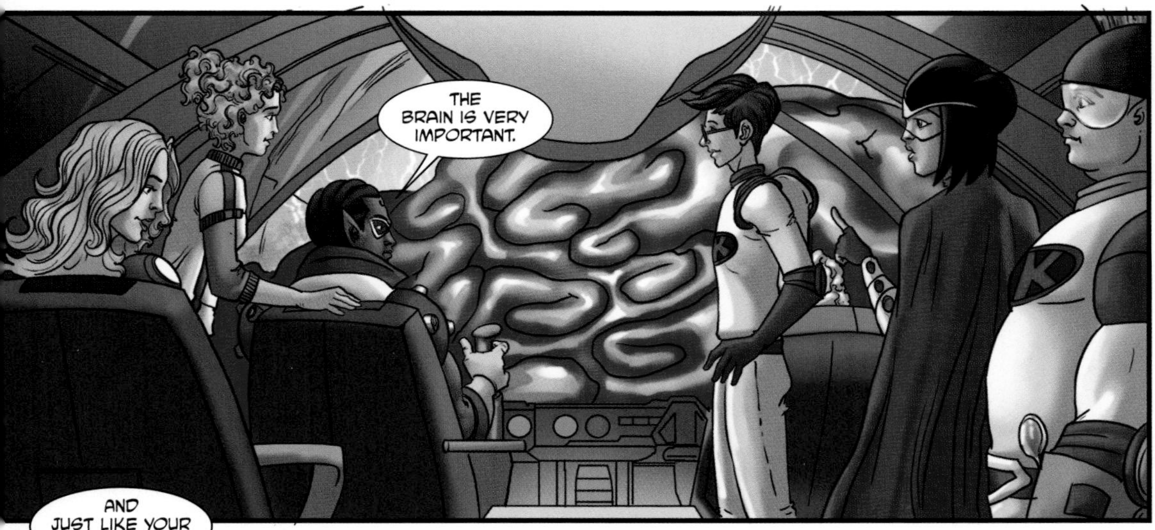
THE BRAIN IS VERY IMPORTANT.

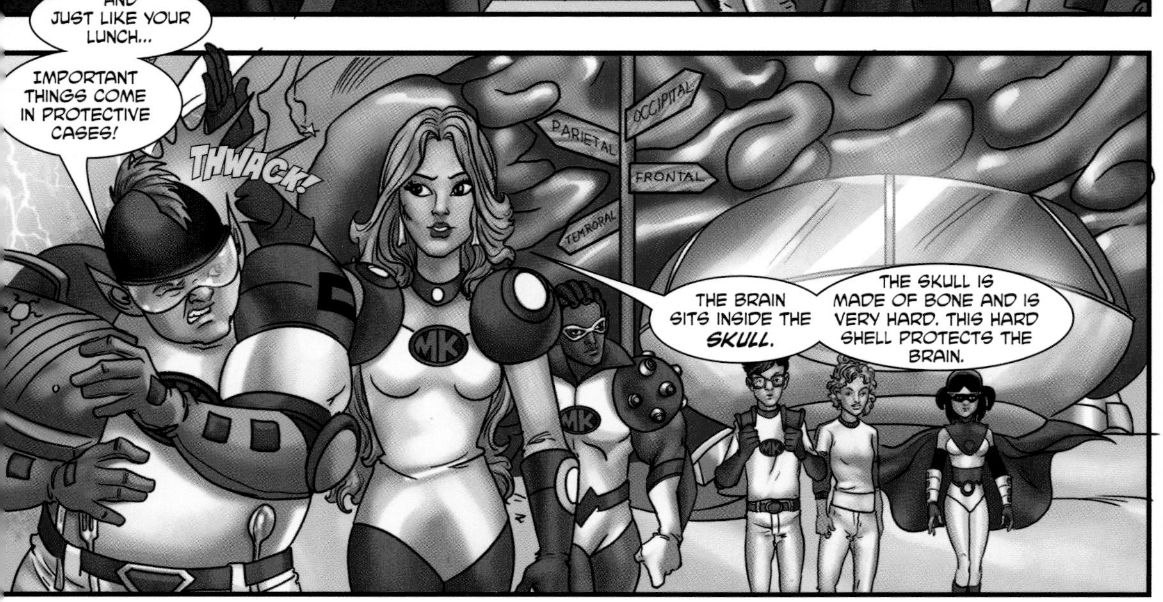
AND JUST LIKE YOUR LUNCH...
IMPORTANT THINGS COME IN PROTECTIVE CASES!
THWACK!
PARIETAL
OCCIPITAL
FRONTAL
TEMPORAL
THE BRAIN SITS INSIDE THE SKULL.
THE SKULL IS MADE OF BONE AND IS VERY HARD. THIS HARD SHELL PROTECTS THE BRAIN.

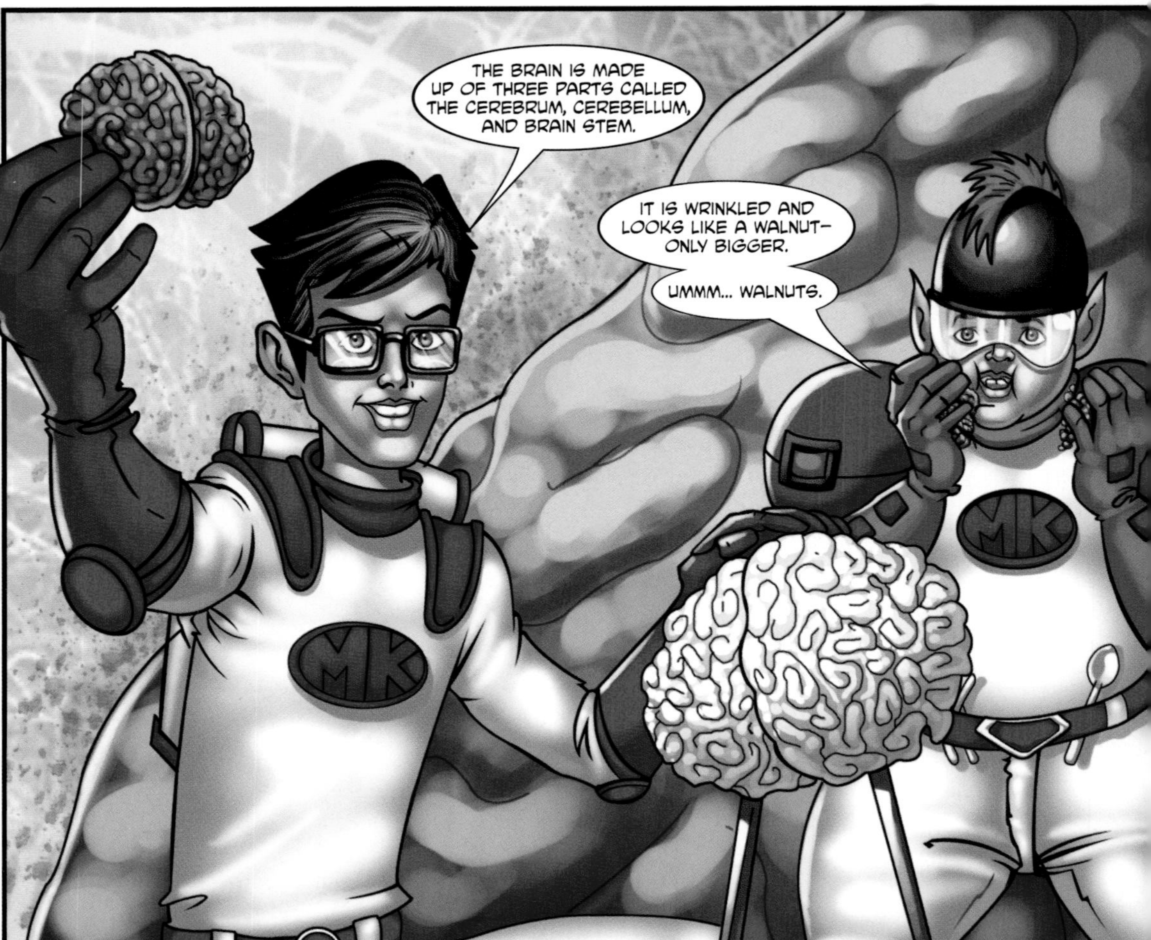
THE BRAIN IS MADE UP OF THREE PARTS CALLED THE CEREBRUM, CEREBELLUM, AND BRAIN STEM.
IT IS WRINKLED AND LOOKS LIKE A WALNUT–ONLY BIGGER.
UMMM... WALNUTS.

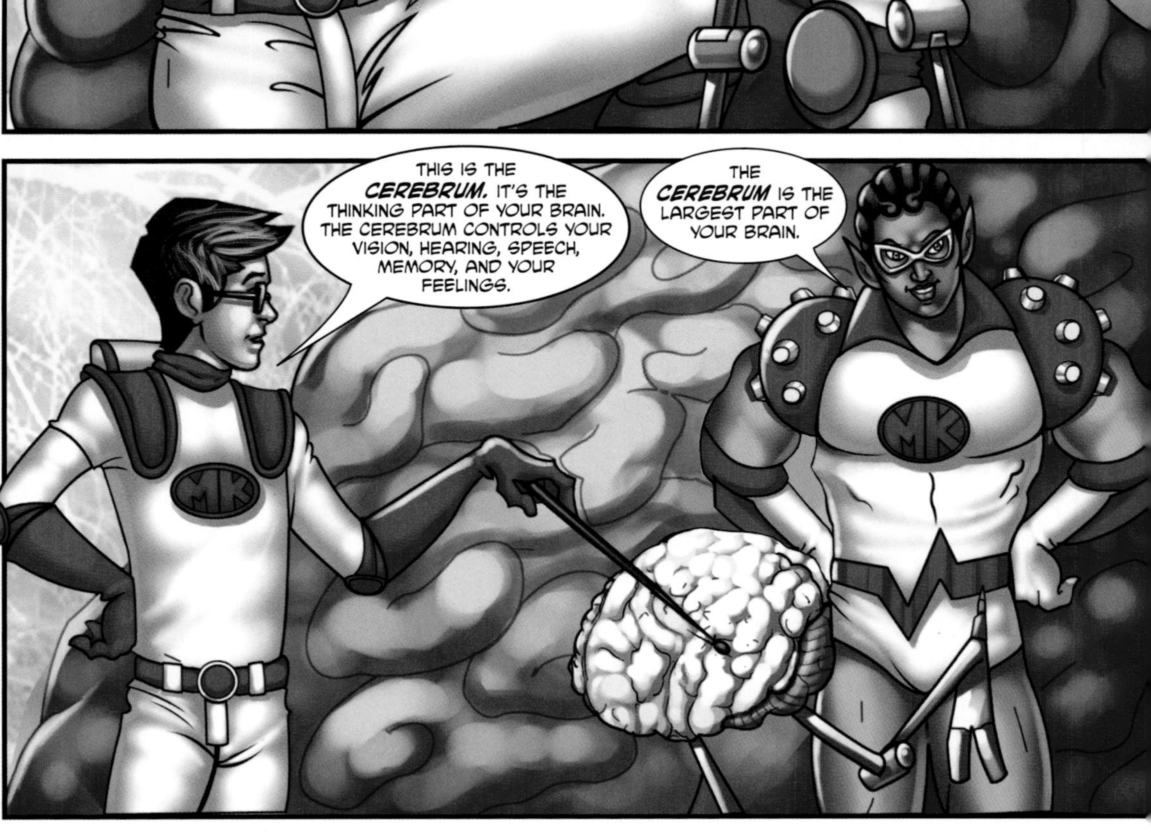
THIS IS THE ***CEREBRUM.*** IT'S THE THINKING PART OF YOUR BRAIN. THE CEREBRUM CONTROLS YOUR VISION, HEARING, SPEECH, MEMORY, AND YOUR FEELINGS.
THE ***CEREBRUM*** IS THE LARGEST PART OF YOUR BRAIN.
MK
MK
MK
MK

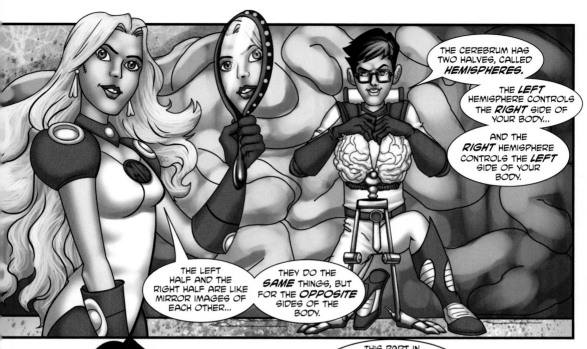

THE CEREBRUM HAS TWO HALVES, CALLED *HEMISPHERES.*

THE *LEFT* HEMISPHERE CONTROLS THE *RIGHT* SIDE OF YOUR BODY...

AND THE *RIGHT* HEMISPHERE CONTROLS THE *LEFT* SIDE OF YOUR BODY.

THE LEFT HALF AND THE RIGHT HALF ARE LIKE MIRROR IMAGES OF EACH OTHER...

THEY DO THE *SAME* THINGS, BUT FOR THE *OPPOSITE* SIDES OF THE BODY.

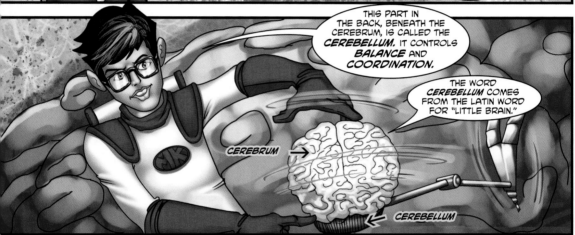

THIS PART IN THE BACK, BENEATH THE CEREBRUM, IS CALLED THE *CEREBELLUM.* IT CONTROLS *BALANCE* AND *COORDINATION.*

THE WORD *CEREBELLUM* COMES FROM THE LATIN WORD FOR "LITTLE BRAIN."

CEREBRUM

CEREBELLUM

THIS PART AT THE BOTTOM IS CALLED THE BRAIN STEM. IT CONTROLS THE AUTOMATIC SYSTEMS IN YOUR BODY LIKE BREATHING AND DIGESTION.

THE BRAIN STEM CONNECTS THE REST OF THE BRAIN TO THE SPINAL CORD.

CEREBRUM

CEREBELLUM

BRAIN STEM

MY BRAINSTEM MUST BE IN *OVERDRIVE!*

CLICK

LET'S GO INSIDE THE BRAIN AND TAKE A CLOSER LOOK!

INSIDE THE BRAIN...

AMAZING!

YOUR BRAIN WORKS BY SENDING *MESSAGES* TO THE REST OF YOUR BODY—TELLING IT WHAT TO DO.

RUN

SWALLOW

SCRATCH MY NOSE

MOVE LEFT FOOT

YOUR BRAIN IS MADE UP OF *BILLIONS* OF BRAIN CELLS.

THE MEDICAL TERM FOR BRAIN CELL IS *NEURON*.

HERE, TAKE A LOOK...

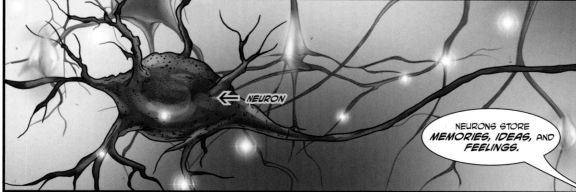

← NEURON

NEURONS STORE *MEMORIES, IDEAS,* AND *FEELINGS.*

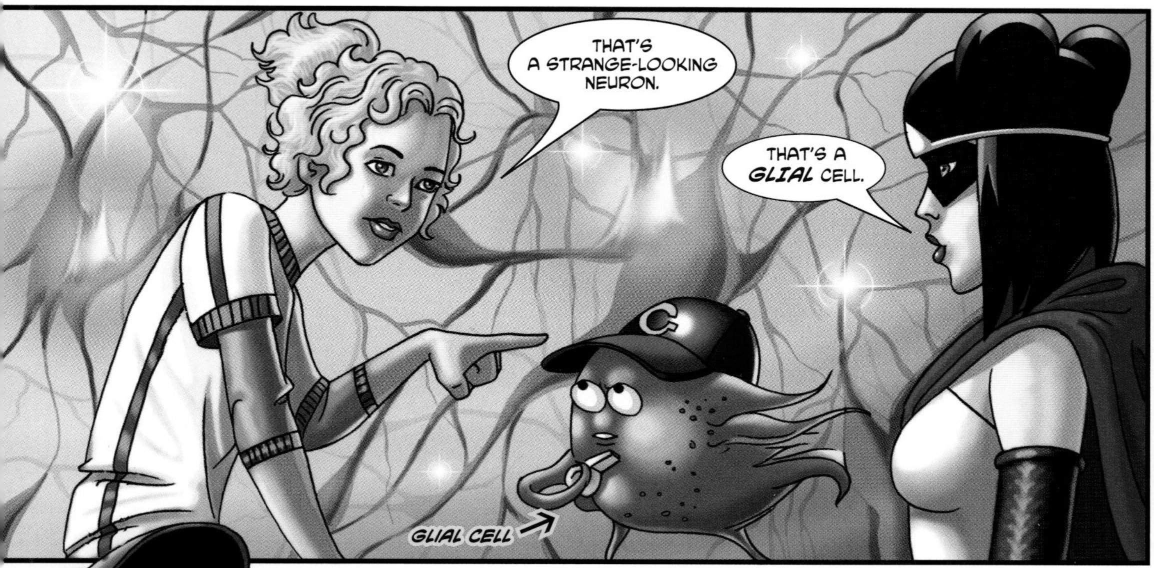
THAT'S A STRANGE-LOOKING NEURON.
THAT'S A GLIAL CELL.
GLIAL CELL

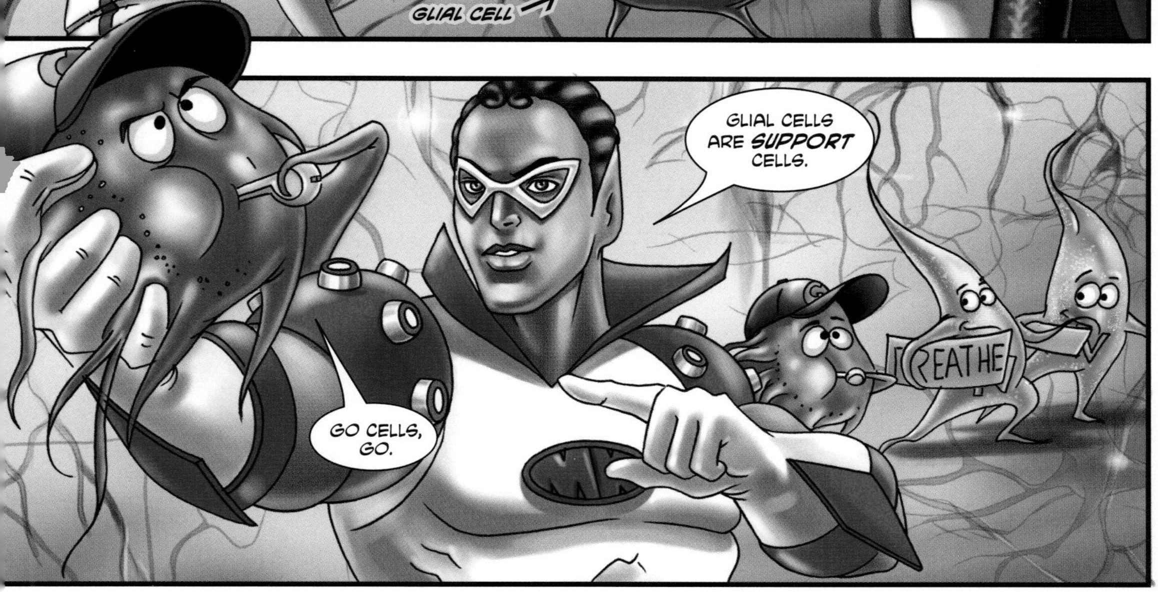
GLIAL CELLS ARE SUPPORT CELLS.
GO CELLS, GO.

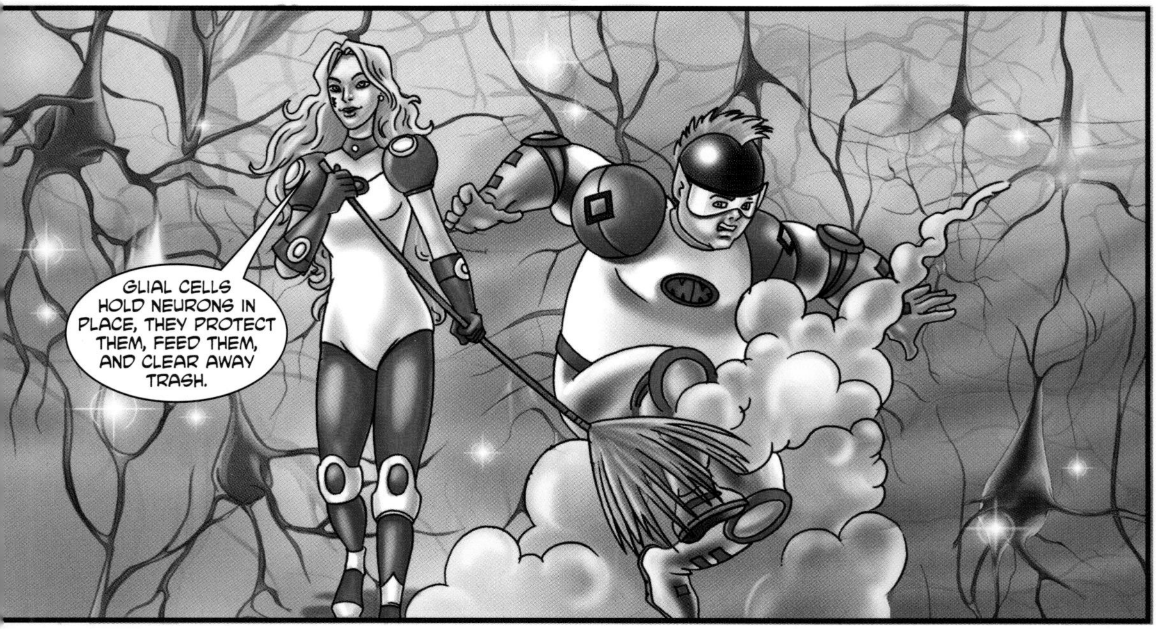
GLIAL CELLS HOLD NEURONS IN PLACE, THEY PROTECT THEM, FEED THEM, AND CLEAR AWAY TRASH.

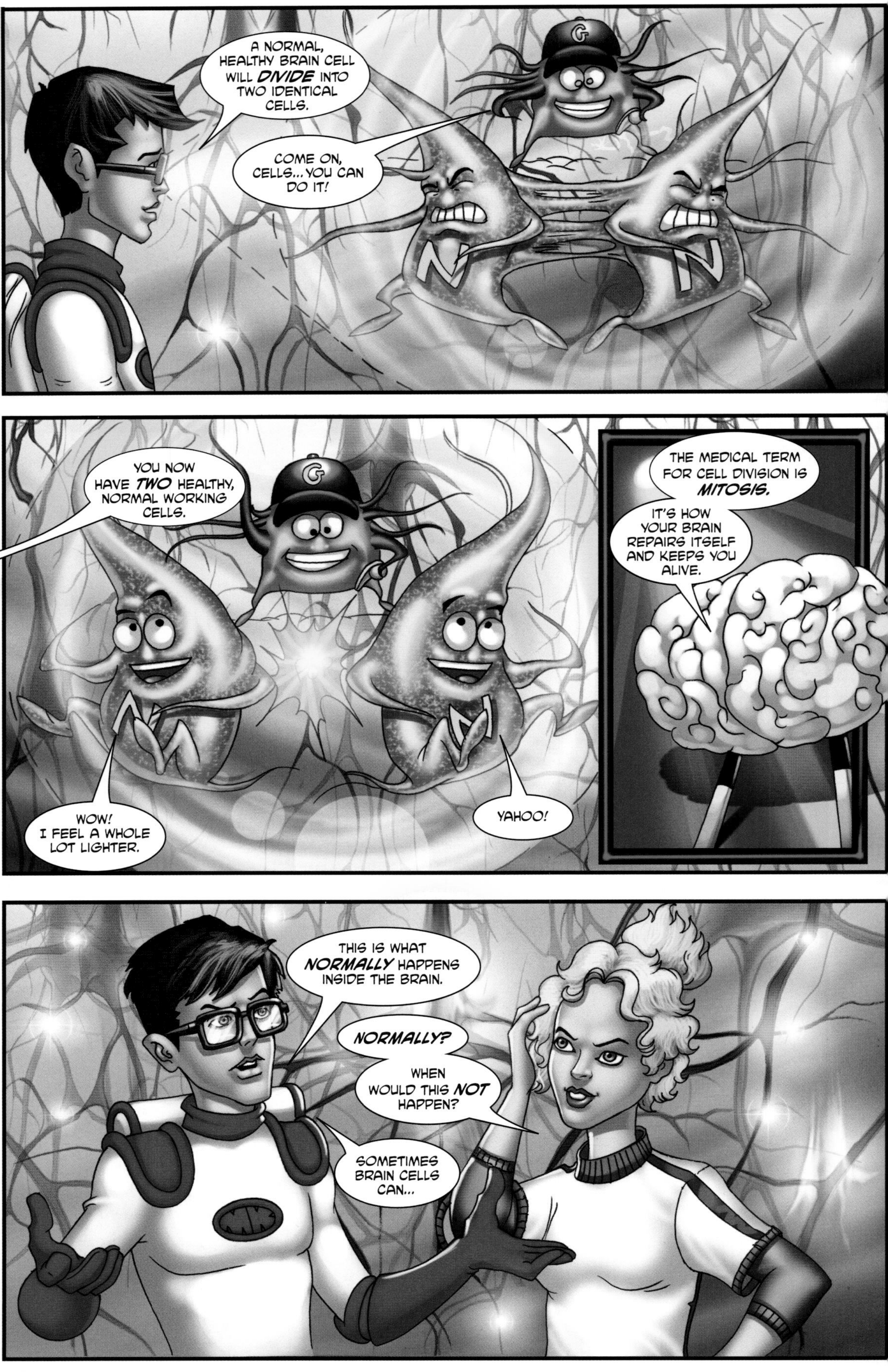
A NORMAL, HEALTHY BRAIN CELL WILL DIVIDE INTO TWO IDENTICAL CELLS.
COME ON, CELLS... YOU CAN DO IT!
YOU NOW HAVE TWO HEALTHY, NORMAL WORKING CELLS.
WOW! I FEEL A WHOLE LOT LIGHTER.
YAHOO!
THE MEDICAL TERM FOR CELL DIVISION IS MITOSIS.
IT'S HOW YOUR BRAIN REPAIRS ITSELF AND KEEPS YOU ALIVE.
THIS IS WHAT NORMALLY HAPPENS INSIDE THE BRAIN.
NORMALLY?
WHEN WOULD THIS NOT HAPPEN?
SOMETIMES BRAIN CELLS CAN...

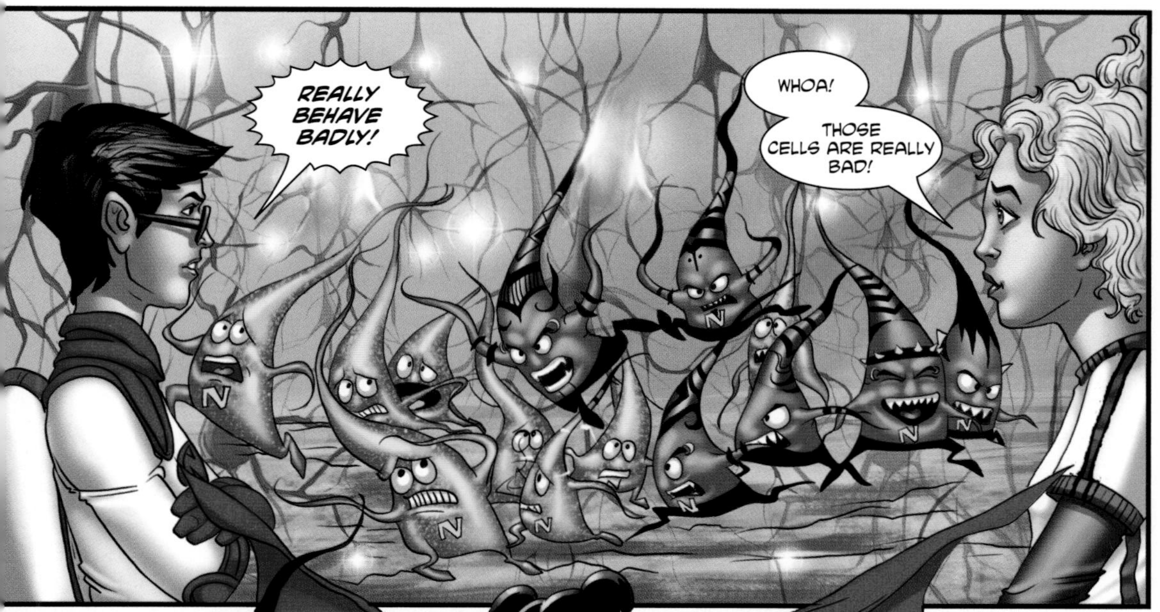
REALLY BEHAVE BADLY!
WHOA!
THOSE CELLS ARE REALLY BAD!

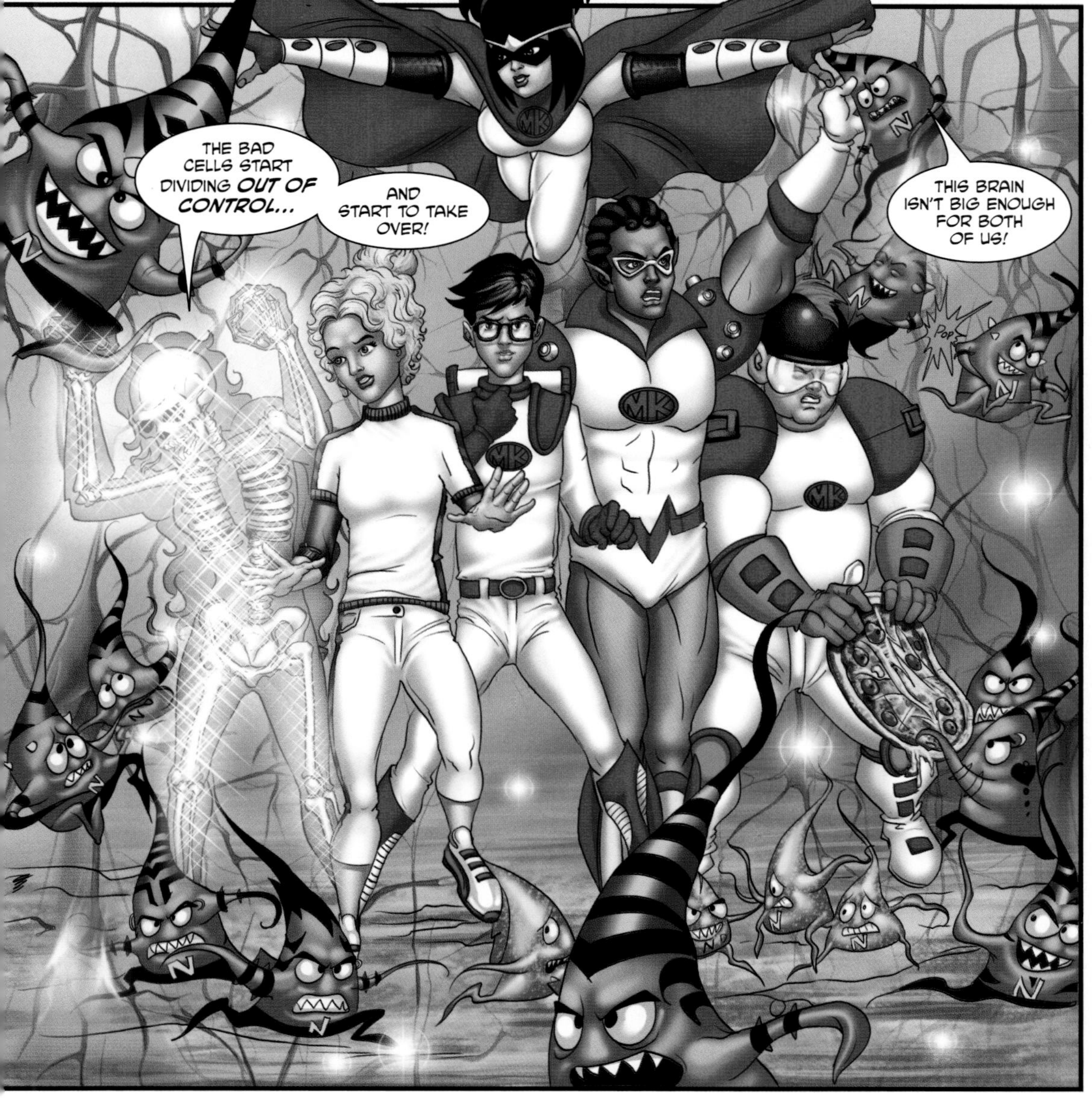
THE BAD CELLS START DIVIDING OUT OF CONTROL...
AND START TO TAKE OVER!
THIS BRAIN ISN'T BIG ENOUGH FOR BOTH OF US!
POP

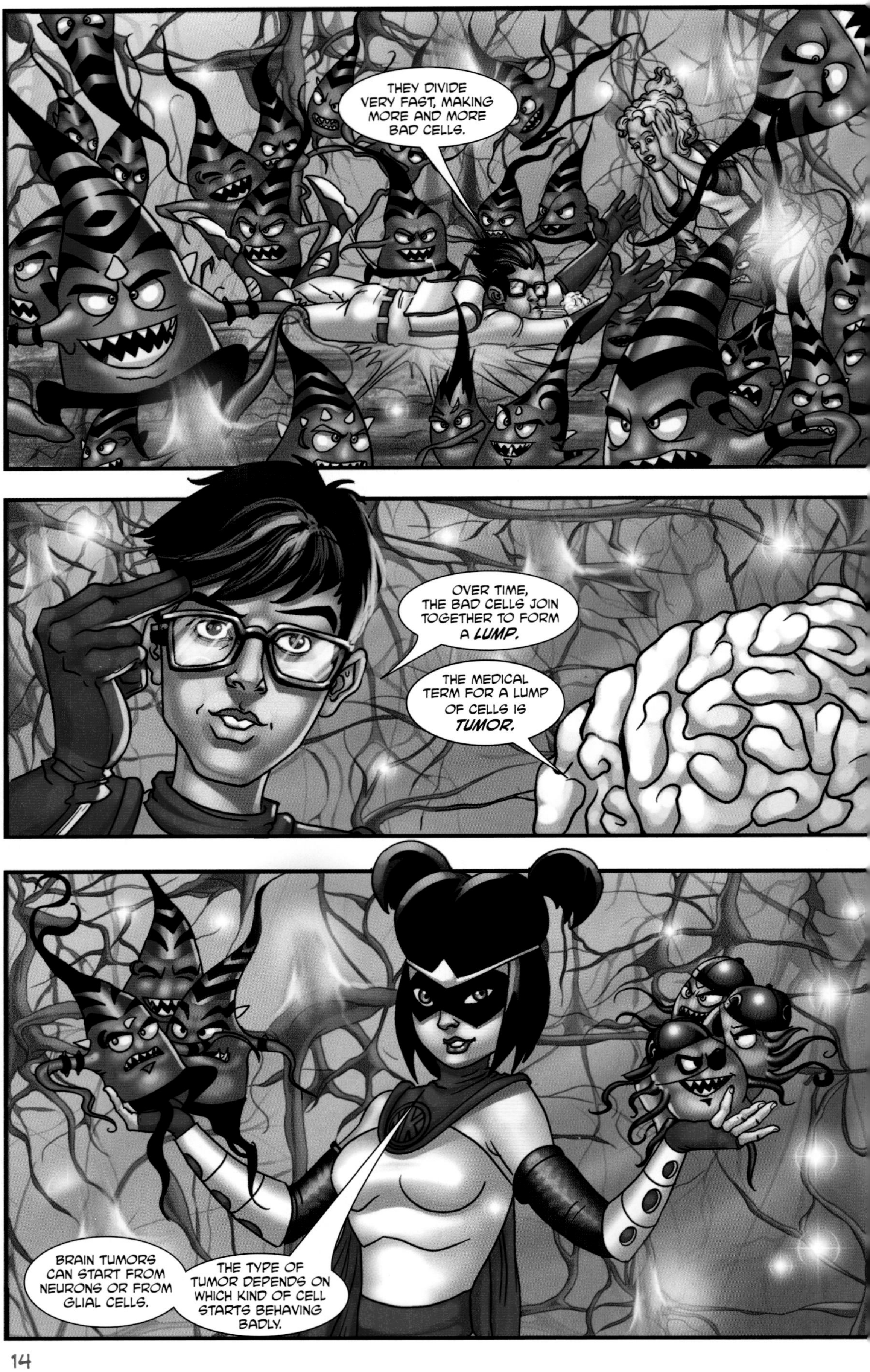
THEY DIVIDE VERY FAST, MAKING MORE AND MORE BAD CELLS.
OVER TIME, THE BAD CELLS JOIN TOGETHER TO FORM A *LUMP.*
THE MEDICAL TERM FOR A LUMP OF CELLS IS *TUMOR.*
BRAIN TUMORS CAN START FROM NEURONS OR FROM GLIAL CELLS.
THE TYPE OF TUMOR DEPENDS ON WHICH KIND OF CELL STARTS BEHAVING BADLY.

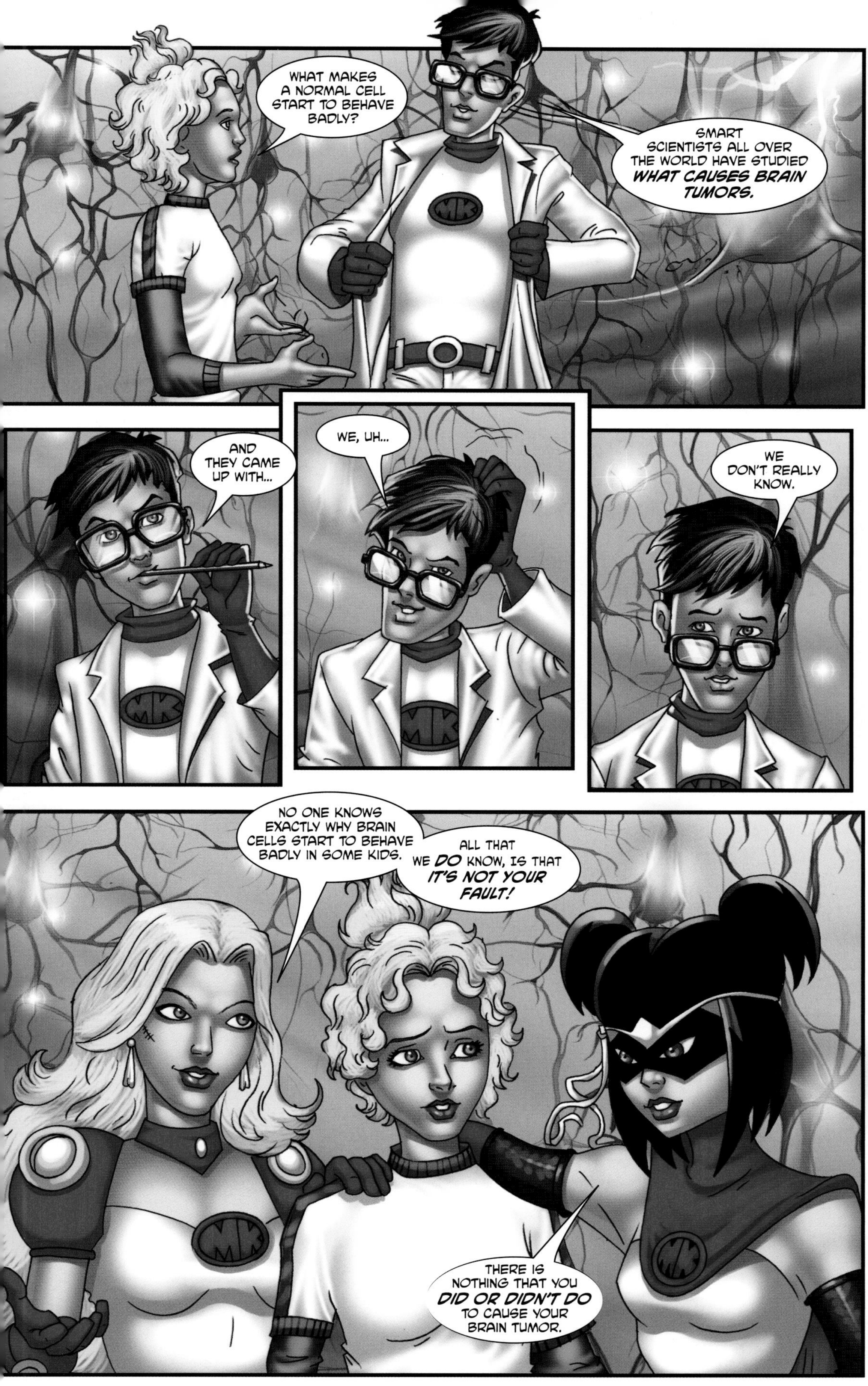
WHAT MAKES A NORMAL CELL START TO BEHAVE BADLY?
SMART SCIENTISTS ALL OVER THE WORLD HAVE STUDIED WHAT CAUSES BRAIN TUMORS.
AND THEY CAME UP WITH...
WE, UH...
WE DON'T REALLY KNOW.
NO ONE KNOWS EXACTLY WHY BRAIN CELLS START TO BEHAVE BADLY IN SOME KIDS.
ALL THAT WE DO KNOW, IS THAT IT'S NOT YOUR FAULT!
THERE IS NOTHING THAT YOU DID OR DIDN'T DO TO CAUSE YOUR BRAIN TUMOR.

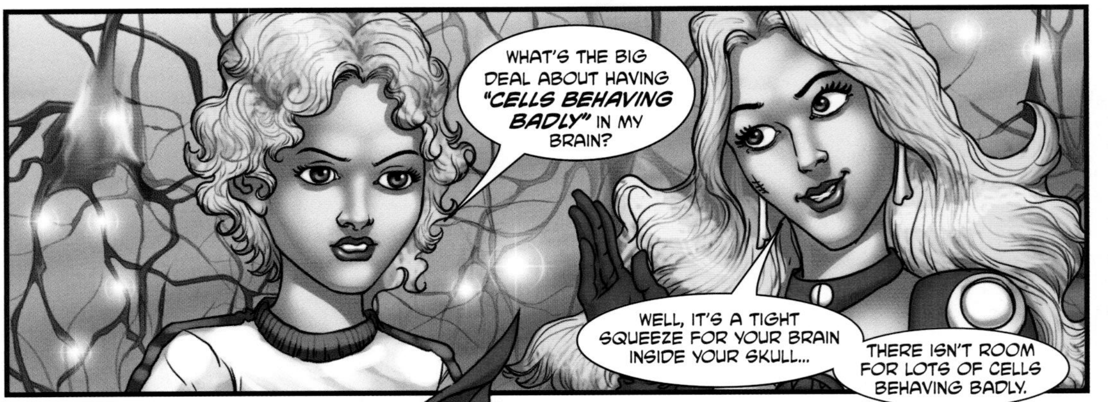
WHAT'S THE BIG DEAL ABOUT HAVING "CELLS BEHAVING BADLY" IN MY BRAIN?
WELL, IT'S A TIGHT SQUEEZE FOR YOUR BRAIN INSIDE YOUR SKULL...
THERE ISN'T ROOM FOR LOTS OF CELLS BEHAVING BADLY.

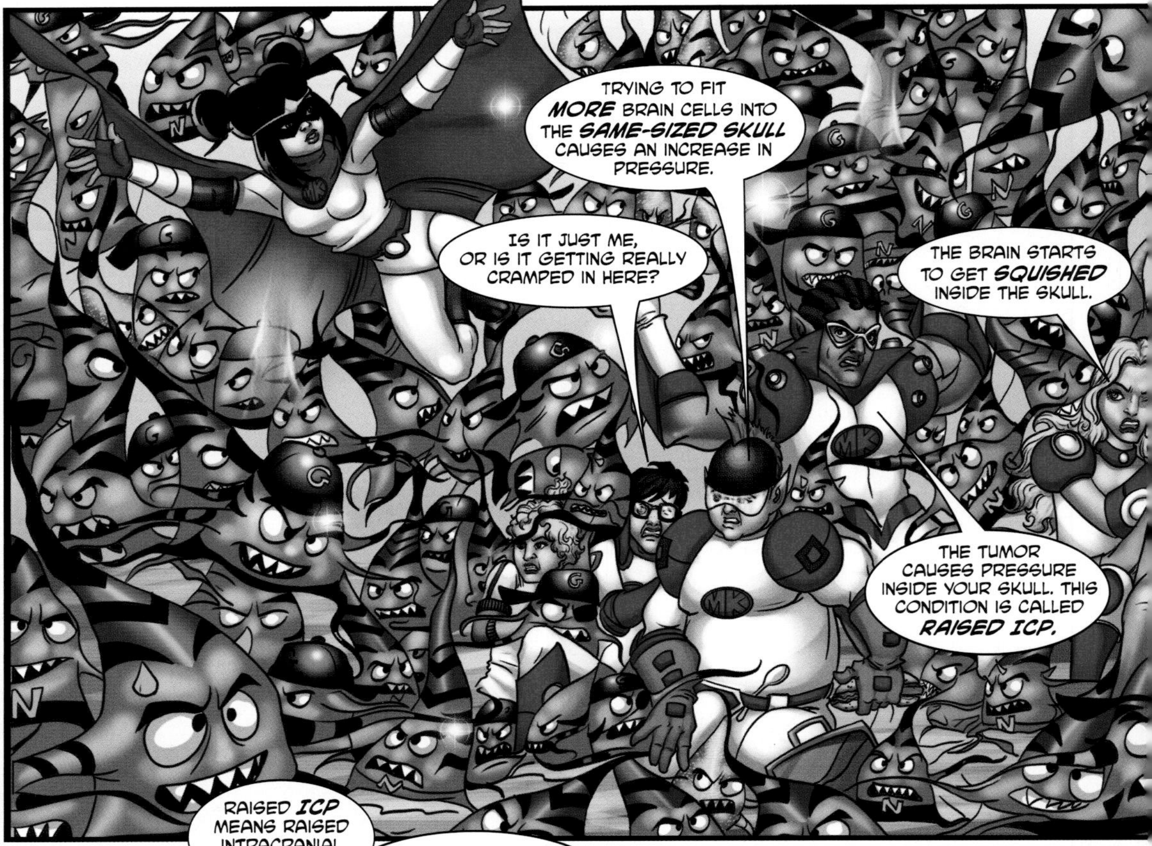
TRYING TO FIT MORE BRAIN CELLS INTO THE SAME-SIZED SKULL CAUSES AN INCREASE IN PRESSURE.
IS IT JUST ME, OR IS IT GETTING REALLY CRAMPED IN HERE?
THE BRAIN STARTS TO GET SQUISHED INSIDE THE SKULL.
THE TUMOR CAUSES PRESSURE INSIDE YOUR SKULL. THIS CONDITION IS CALLED RAISED ICP.

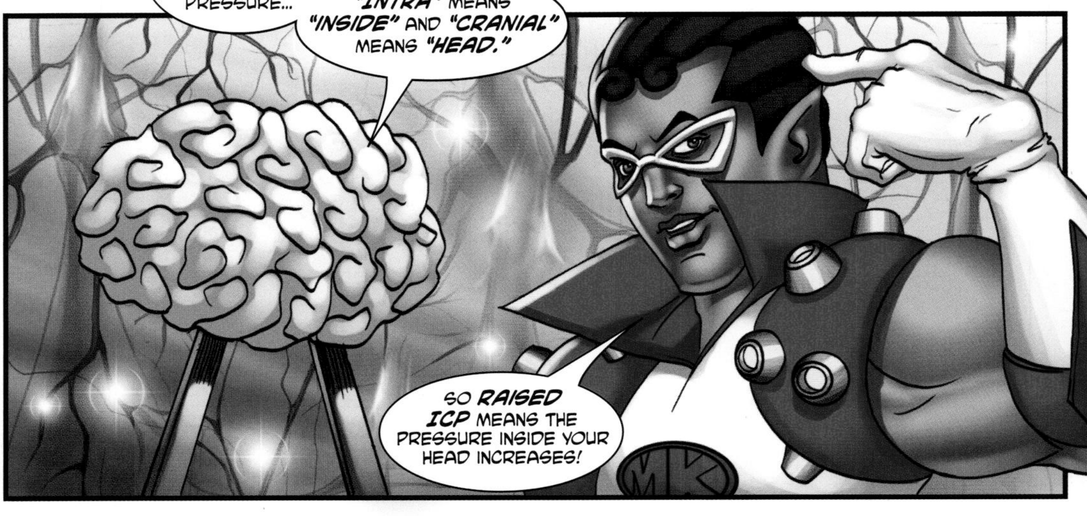
RAISED ICP MEANS RAISED INTRACRANIAL PRESSURE...
"INTRA" MEANS "INSIDE" AND "CRANIAL" MEANS "HEAD."
SO RAISED ICP MEANS THE PRESSURE INSIDE YOUR HEAD INCREASES!

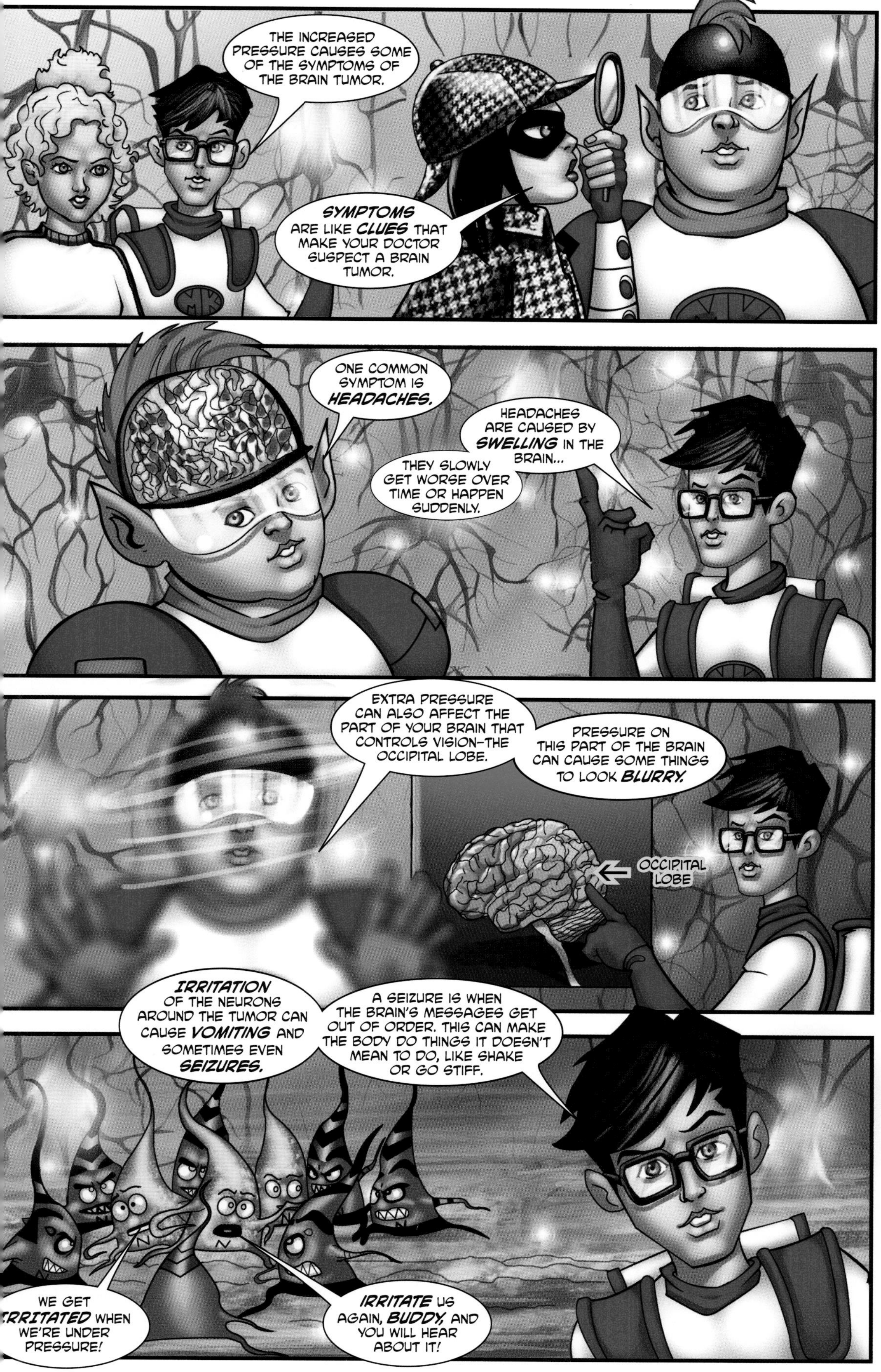
THE INCREASED PRESSURE CAUSES SOME OF THE SYMPTOMS OF THE BRAIN TUMOR.
SYMPTOMS ARE LIKE CLUES THAT MAKE YOUR DOCTOR SUSPECT A BRAIN TUMOR.
ONE COMMON SYMPTOM IS HEADACHES.
HEADACHES ARE CAUSED BY SWELLING IN THE BRAIN...
THEY SLOWLY GET WORSE OVER TIME OR HAPPEN SUDDENLY.
EXTRA PRESSURE CAN ALSO AFFECT THE PART OF YOUR BRAIN THAT CONTROLS VISION—THE OCCIPITAL LOBE.
PRESSURE ON THIS PART OF THE BRAIN CAN CAUSE SOME THINGS TO LOOK BLURRY.
OCCIPITAL LOBE
IRRITATION OF THE NEURONS AROUND THE TUMOR CAN CAUSE VOMITING AND SOMETIMES EVEN SEIZURES.
A SEIZURE IS WHEN THE BRAIN'S MESSAGES GET OUT OF ORDER. THIS CAN MAKE THE BODY DO THINGS IT DOESN'T MEAN TO DO, LIKE SHAKE OR GO STIFF.
WE GET RRITATED WHEN WE'RE UNDER PRESSURE!
IRRITATE US AGAIN, BUDDY, AND YOU WILL HEAR ABOUT IT!

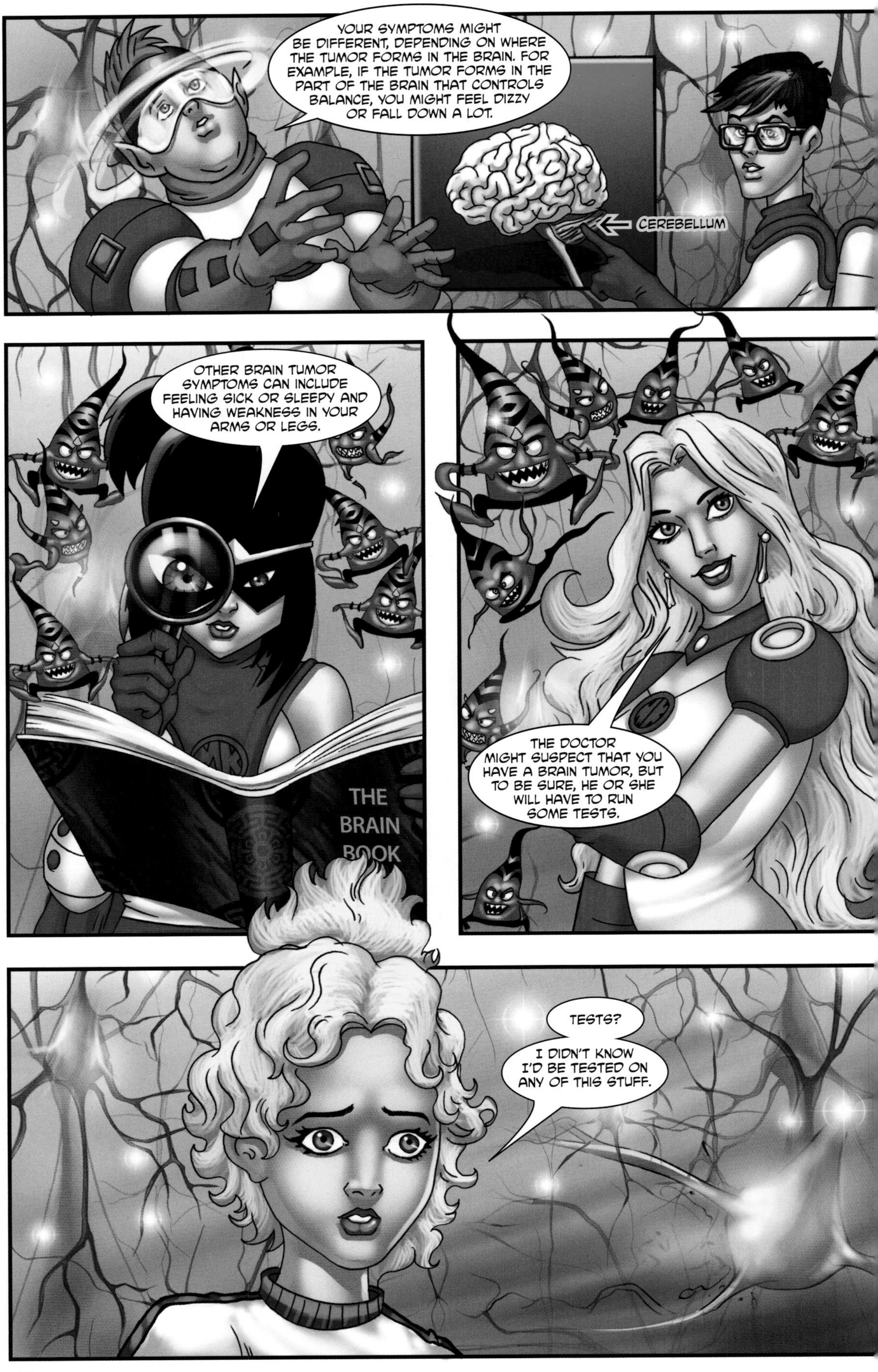

YOUR SYMPTOMS MIGHT BE DIFFERENT, DEPENDING ON WHERE THE TUMOR FORMS IN THE BRAIN. FOR EXAMPLE, IF THE TUMOR FORMS IN THE PART OF THE BRAIN THAT CONTROLS BALANCE, YOU MIGHT FEEL DIZZY OR FALL DOWN A LOT.
CEREBELLUM
OTHER BRAIN TUMOR SYMPTOMS CAN INCLUDE FEELING SICK OR SLEEPY AND HAVING WEAKNESS IN YOUR ARMS OR LEGS.
THE BRAIN BOOK
THE DOCTOR MIGHT SUSPECT THAT YOU HAVE A BRAIN TUMOR, BUT TO BE SURE, HE OR SHE WILL HAVE TO RUN SOME TESTS.
TESTS?
I DIDN'T KNOW I'D BE TESTED ON ANY OF THIS STUFF.

HI, I'M RORY, THE RADIOLOGIC TECHNOLOGIST.
I CAN USE SPECIAL MACHINES TO TAKE PICTURES OF YOUR BRAIN.
PICTURES OF MY BRAIN...
TAKEN FROM OUTSIDE OF MY HEAD?!
WOW, THAT'S AMAZING!
A CT SCANNER USES X-RAYS TO TAKE PICTURES OF YOUR BRAIN.
IT CAN'T MAKE POPCORN BY THE WAY...
I TRIED.
THESE PICTURES CAN SHOW US IF THERE IS A TUMOR, WHERE IT IS IN THE BRAIN, AND HOW BIG IT IS.
THE MACHINE TAKES MANY SCANS OF YOUR BRAIN FROM DIFFERENT ANGLES AND COMBINES THEM INTO PICTURES.
HOW DOES IT DO THAT?
THE X-RAYS PASS THROUGH THE SOFTER PARTS OF YOUR BRAIN, BUT REFLECT OFF THE HARDER PARTS...
LIKE THE SHAPE OF THE BONES NEAR THE TUMOR.
CT STANDS FOR COMPUTED TOMOGRAPHY.
THERE IT IS...
TUMOR LOCATED!

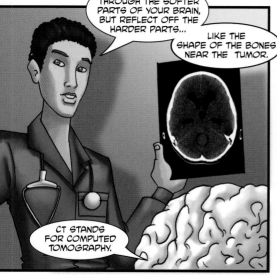

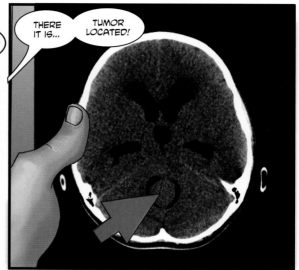

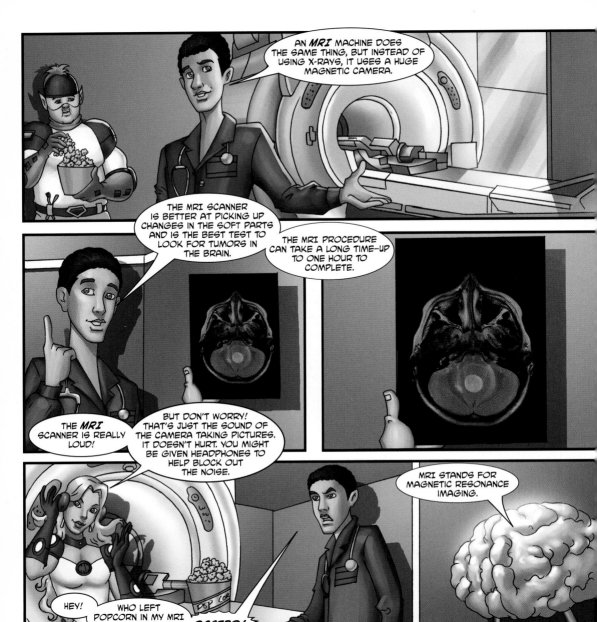

AN *MRI* MACHINE DOES THE SAME THING, BUT INSTEAD OF USING X-RAYS, IT USES A HUGE MAGNETIC CAMERA.

THE MRI SCANNER IS BETTER AT PICKING UP CHANGES IN THE SOFT PARTS AND IS THE BEST TEST TO LOOK FOR TUMORS IN THE BRAIN.

THE MRI PROCEDURE CAN TAKE A LONG TIME–UP TO ONE HOUR TO COMPLETE.

THE *MRI* SCANNER IS REALLY LOUD!

BUT DON'T WORRY! THAT'S JUST THE SOUND OF THE CAMERA TAKING PICTURES. IT DOESN'T HURT. YOU MIGHT BE GIVEN HEADPHONES TO HELP BLOCK OUT THE NOISE.

MRI STANDS FOR MAGNETIC RESONANCE IMAGING.

HEY!

WHO LEFT POPCORN IN MY MRI MACHINE?!

GASTRO!

CT AND MRI SCANS ARE GREAT FOR TELLING US WHERE THE TUMOR IS AND HOW BIG IT IS,

BUT WE STILL NEED TO FIND OUT WHAT KIND OF TUMOR IT IS.

TO LEARN WHAT TYPE OF TUMOR IT IS, YOUR DOCTOR WILL DO A BIOPSY.

GOT HIM!

LET ME GO!!!

RELEASE ME!!

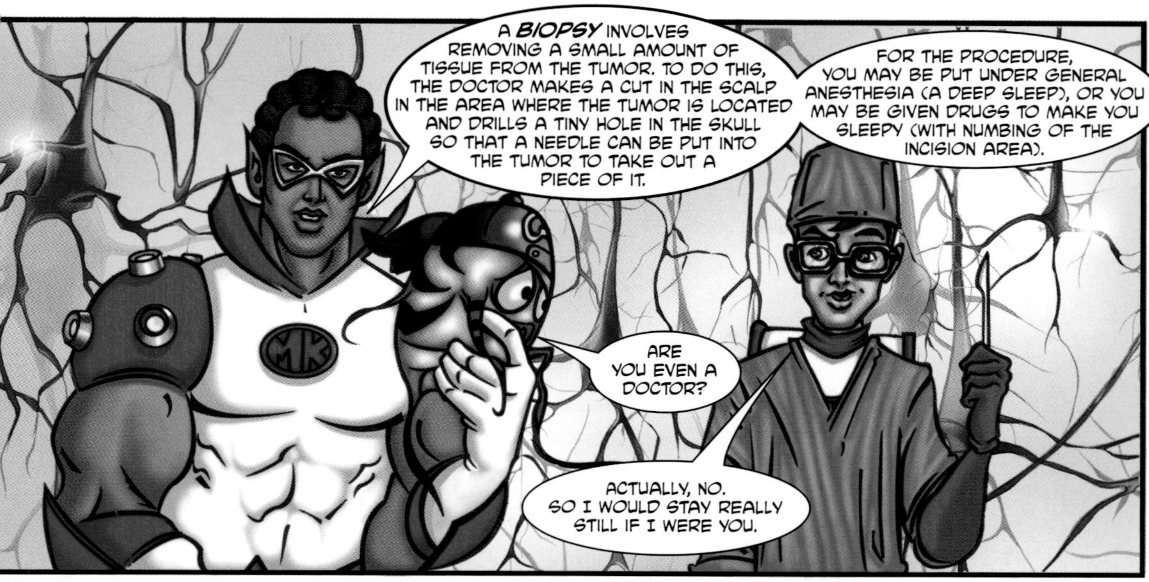
A **BIOPSY** INVOLVES REMOVING A SMALL AMOUNT OF TISSUE FROM THE TUMOR. TO DO THIS, THE DOCTOR MAKES A CUT IN THE SCALP IN THE AREA WHERE THE TUMOR IS LOCATED AND DRILLS A TINY HOLE IN THE SKULL SO THAT A NEEDLE CAN BE PUT INTO THE TUMOR TO TAKE OUT A PIECE OF IT.
FOR THE PROCEDURE, YOU MAY BE PUT UNDER GENERAL ANESTHESIA (A DEEP SLEEP), OR YOU MAY BE GIVEN DRUGS TO MAKE YOU SLEEPY (WITH NUMBING OF THE INCISION AREA).
ARE YOU EVEN A DOCTOR?
ACTUALLY, NO. SO I WOULD STAY REALLY STILL IF I WERE YOU.

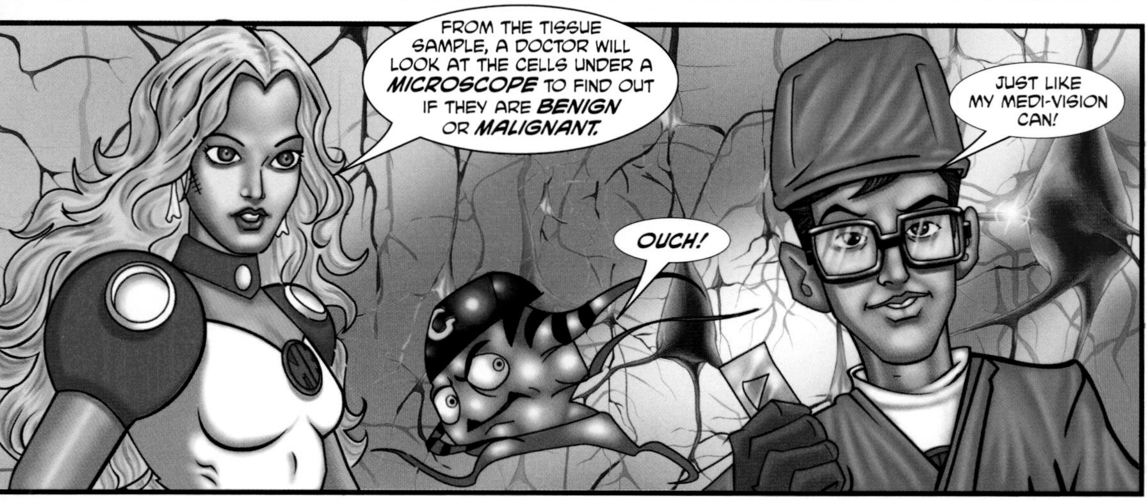
FROM THE TISSUE SAMPLE, A DOCTOR WILL LOOK AT THE CELLS UNDER A **MICROSCOPE** TO FIND OUT IF THEY ARE **BENIGN** OR **MALIGNANT.**
JUST LIKE MY MEDI-VISION CAN!
OUCH!

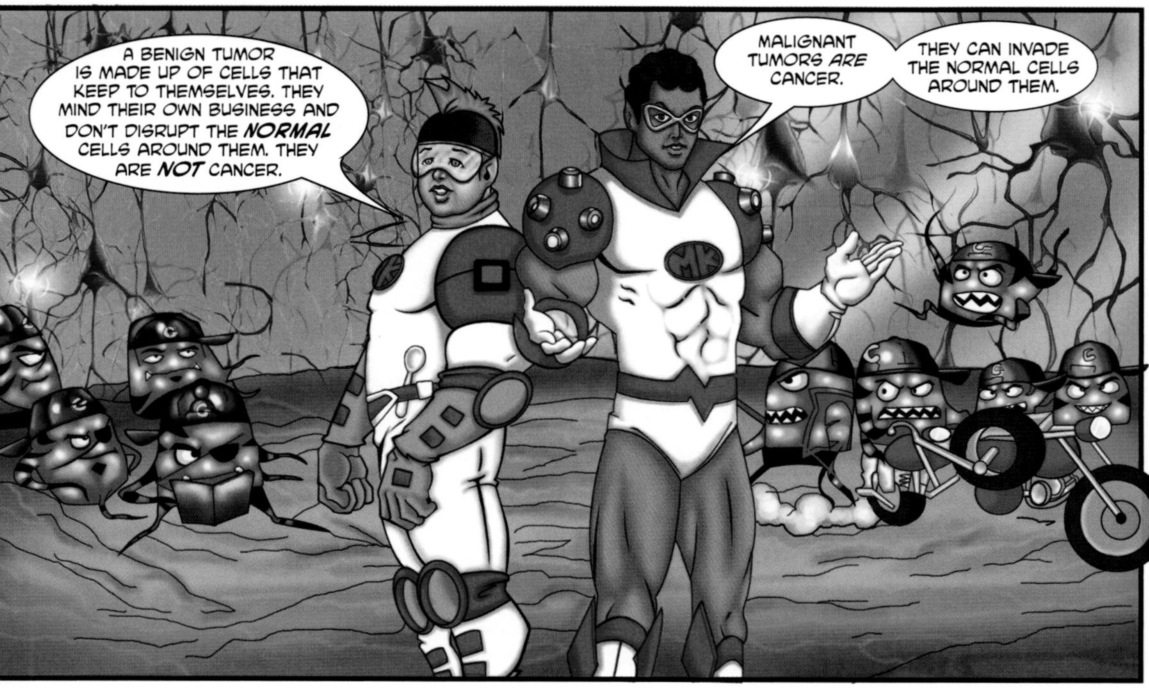
A BENIGN TUMOR IS MADE UP OF CELLS THAT KEEP TO THEMSELVES. THEY MIND THEIR OWN BUSINESS AND DON'T DISRUPT THE **NORMAL** CELLS AROUND THEM. THEY ARE **NOT** CANCER.
MALIGNANT TUMORS *ARE* CANCER.
THEY CAN INVADE THE NORMAL CELLS AROUND THEM.

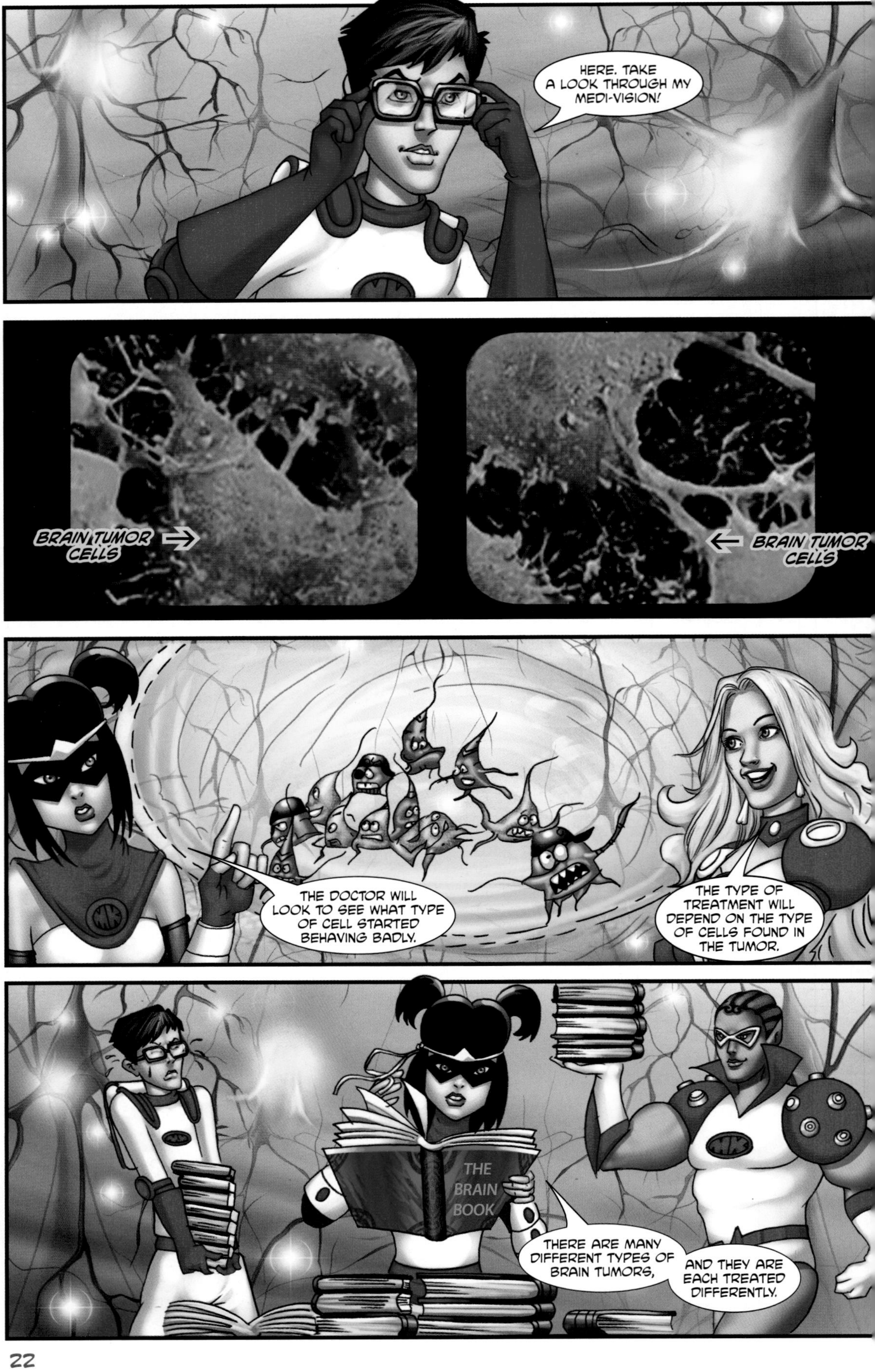

HERE. TAKE A LOOK THROUGH MY MEDI-VISION!
BRAIN TUMOR CELLS
BRAIN TUMOR CELLS
THE DOCTOR WILL LOOK TO SEE WHAT TYPE OF CELL STARTED BEHAVING BADLY.
THE TYPE OF TREATMENT WILL DEPEND ON THE TYPE OF CELLS FOUND IN THE TUMOR.
THE BRAIN BOOK
THERE ARE MANY DIFFERENT TYPES OF BRAIN TUMORS,
AND THEY ARE EACH TREATED DIFFERENTLY.

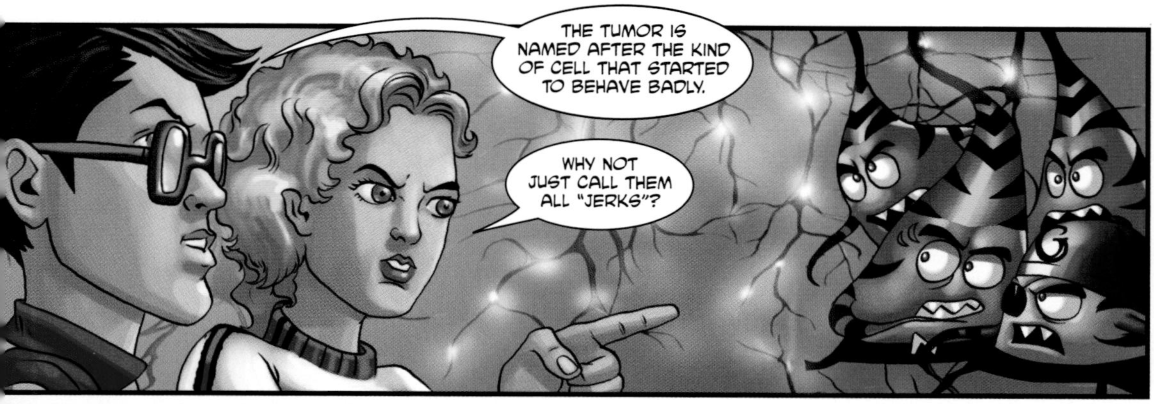
THE TUMOR IS NAMED AFTER THE KIND OF CELL THAT STARTED TO BEHAVE BADLY.
WHY NOT JUST CALL THEM ALL "JERKS"?

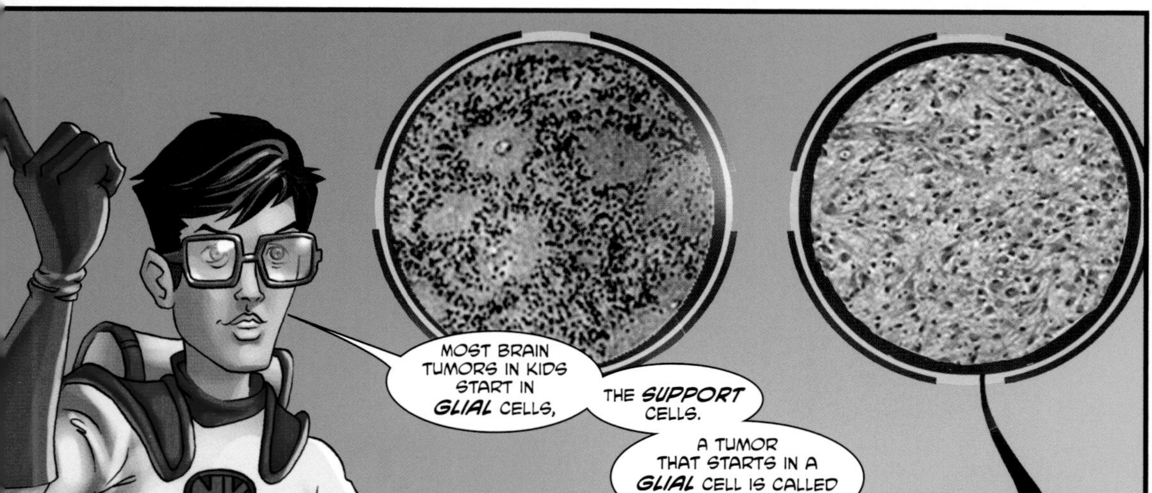
MOST BRAIN TUMORS IN KIDS START IN GLIAL CELLS,
THE SUPPORT CELLS.
A TUMOR THAT STARTS IN A GLIAL CELL IS CALLED A GLIOMA.
THERE ARE TWO MAIN TYPES OF GLIOMAS IN CHILDREN: ASTROCYTOMAS AND EPENDYMOMAS.
ANOTHER TYPE OF BRAIN TUMOR IN KIDS STARTS IN THE CEREBELLUM AND IS CALLED A MEDULLOBLASTOMA.

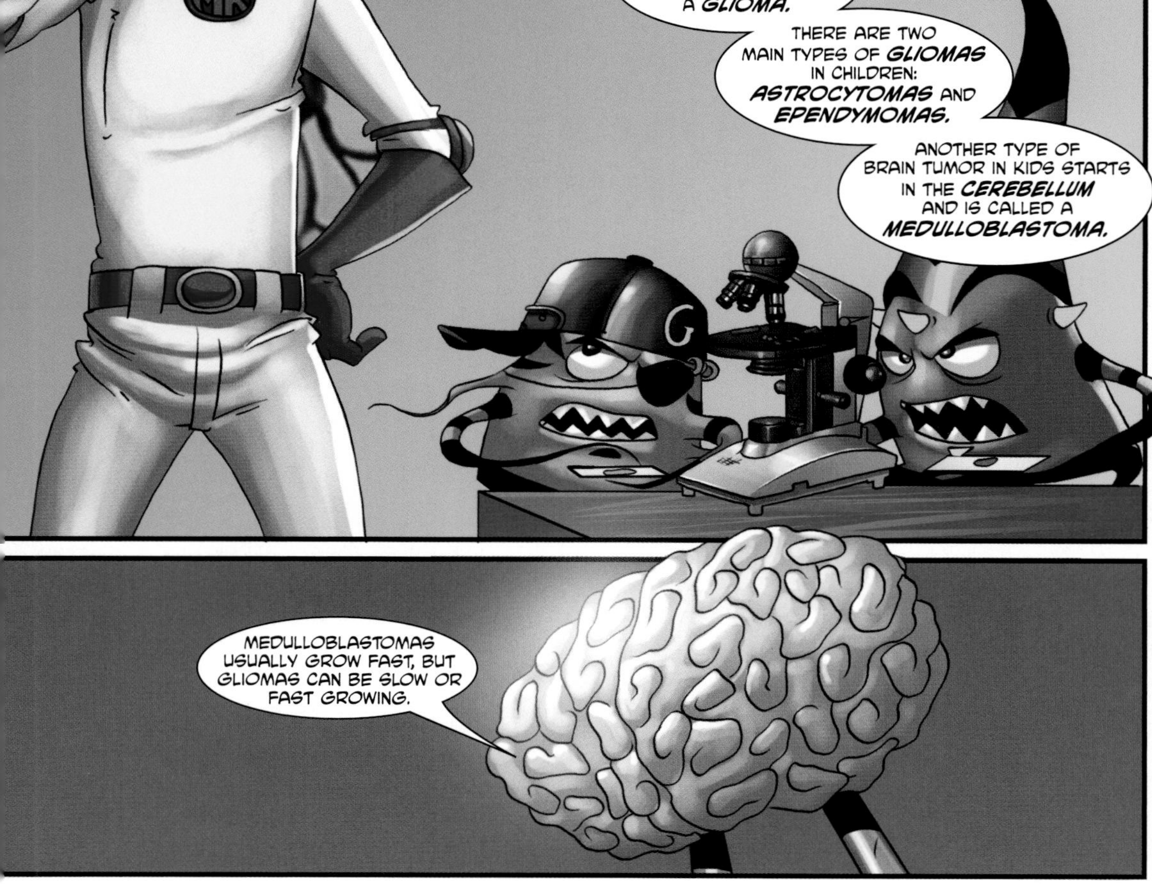
MEDULLOBLASTOMAS USUALLY GROW FAST, BUT GLIOMAS CAN BE SLOW OR FAST GROWING.

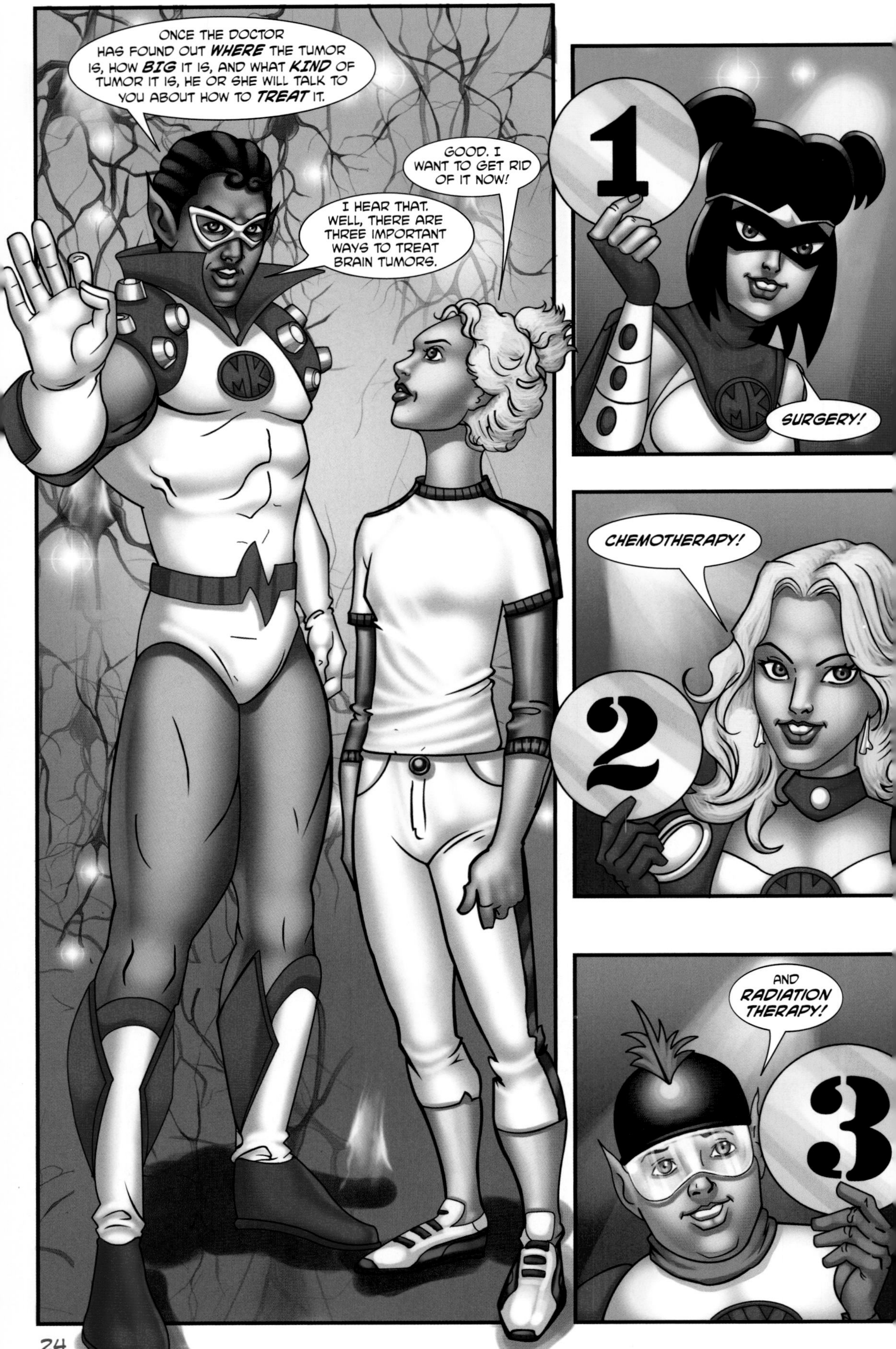
ONCE THE DOCTOR HAS FOUND OUT **WHERE** THE TUMOR IS, HOW **BIG** IT IS, AND WHAT **KIND** OF TUMOR IT IS, HE OR SHE WILL TALK TO YOU ABOUT HOW TO **TREAT** IT.
GOOD. I WANT TO GET RID OF IT NOW!
I HEAR THAT. WELL, THERE ARE THREE IMPORTANT WAYS TO TREAT BRAIN TUMORS.
1
SURGERY!
CHEMOTHERAPY!
2
AND RADIATION THERAPY!
3

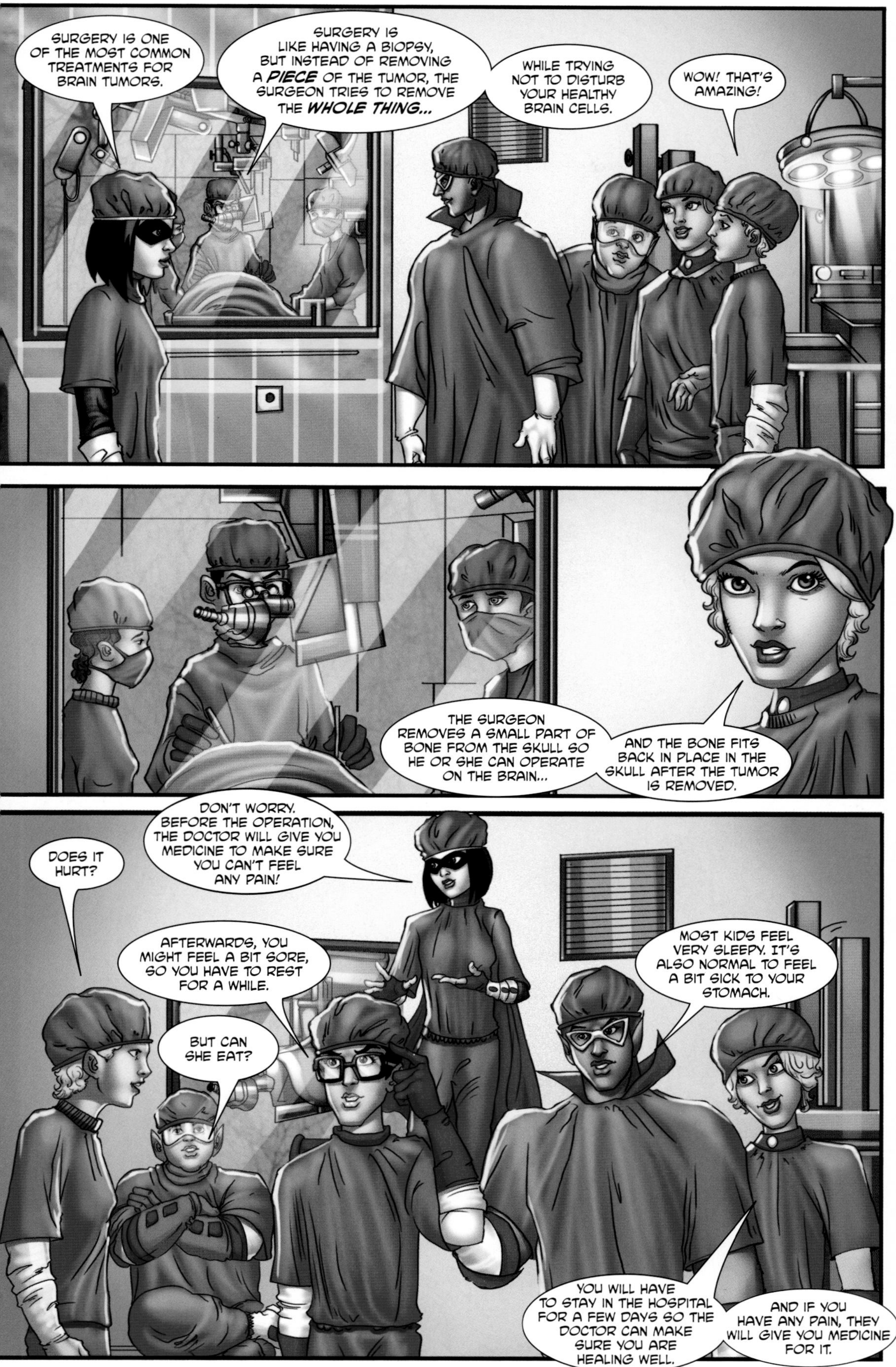
SURGERY IS ONE OF THE MOST COMMON TREATMENTS FOR BRAIN TUMORS.
SURGERY IS LIKE HAVING A BIOPSY, BUT INSTEAD OF REMOVING A PIECE OF THE TUMOR, THE SURGEON TRIES TO REMOVE THE WHOLE THING...
WHILE TRYING NOT TO DISTURB YOUR HEALTHY BRAIN CELLS.
WOW! THAT'S AMAZING!
THE SURGEON REMOVES A SMALL PART OF BONE FROM THE SKULL SO HE OR SHE CAN OPERATE ON THE BRAIN...
AND THE BONE FITS BACK IN PLACE IN THE SKULL AFTER THE TUMOR IS REMOVED.
DOES IT HURT?
DON'T WORRY. BEFORE THE OPERATION, THE DOCTOR WILL GIVE YOU MEDICINE TO MAKE SURE YOU CAN'T FEEL ANY PAIN!
AFTERWARDS, YOU MIGHT FEEL A BIT SORE, SO YOU HAVE TO REST FOR A WHILE.
BUT CAN SHE EAT?
MOST KIDS FEEL VERY SLEEPY. IT'S ALSO NORMAL TO FEEL A BIT SICK TO YOUR STOMACH.
YOU WILL HAVE TO STAY IN THE HOSPITAL FOR A FEW DAYS SO THE DOCTOR CAN MAKE SURE YOU ARE HEALING WELL.
AND IF YOU HAVE ANY PAIN, THEY WILL GIVE YOU MEDICINE FOR IT.

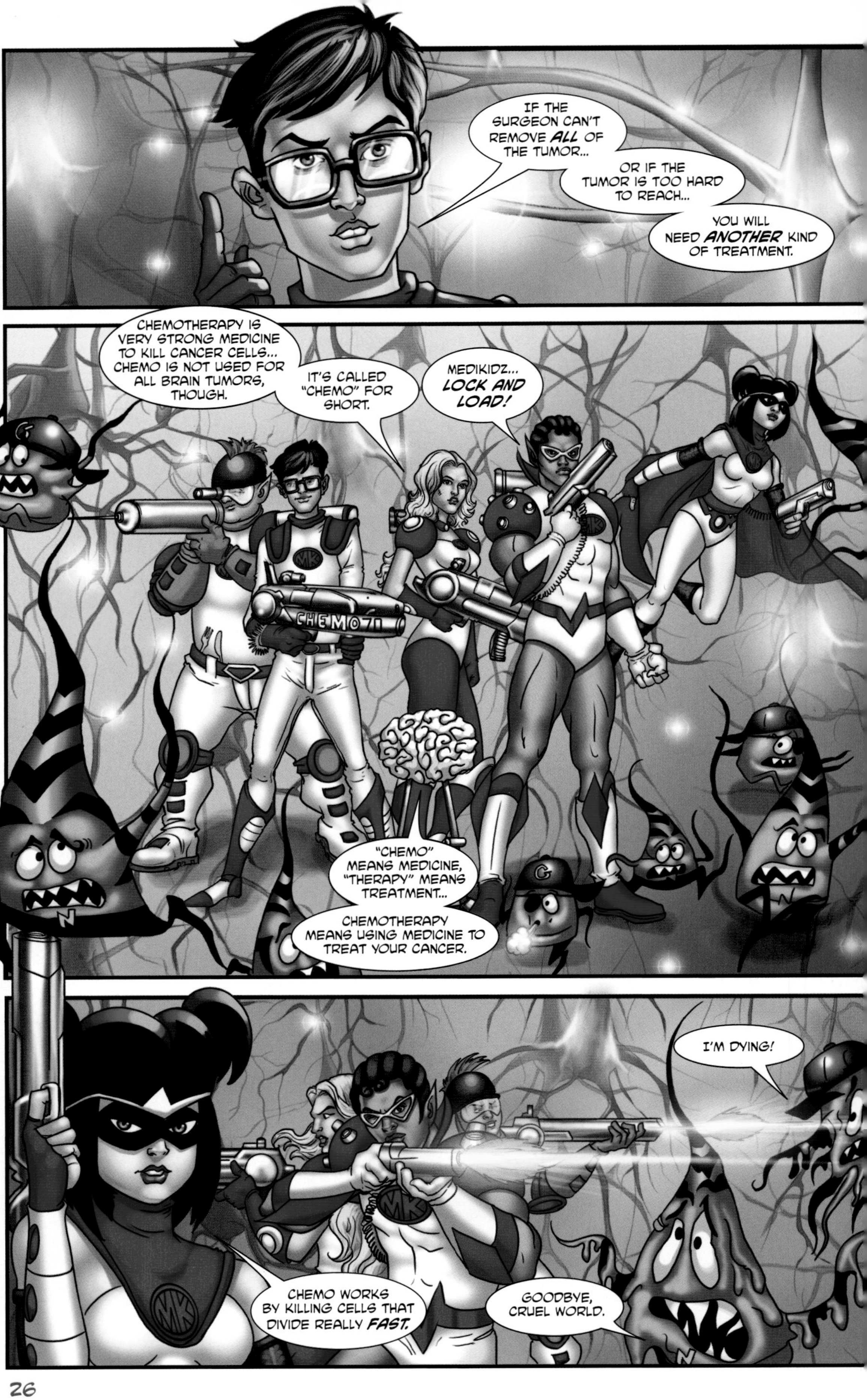
IF THE SURGEON CAN'T REMOVE ALL OF THE TUMOR...
OR IF THE TUMOR IS TOO HARD TO REACH...
YOU WILL NEED ANOTHER KIND OF TREATMENT.
CHEMOTHERAPY IS VERY STRONG MEDICINE TO KILL CANCER CELLS... CHEMO IS NOT USED FOR ALL BRAIN TUMORS, THOUGH.
IT'S CALLED "CHEMO" FOR SHORT.
MEDIKIDZ... LOCK AND LOAD!
CHEMO
"CHEMO" MEANS MEDICINE, "THERAPY" MEANS TREATMENT...
CHEMOTHERAPY MEANS USING MEDICINE TO TREAT YOUR CANCER.
I'M DYING!
CHEMO WORKS BY KILLING CELLS THAT DIVIDE REALLY FAST.
GOODBYE, CRUEL WORLD.

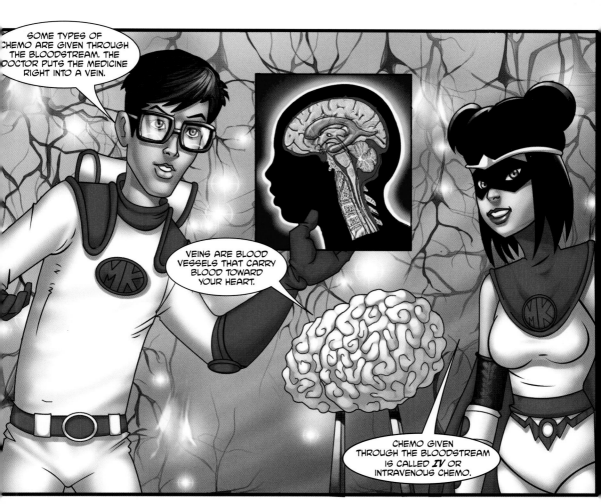

SOME TYPES OF CHEMO ARE GIVEN THROUGH THE BLOODSTREAM. THE DOCTOR PUTS THE MEDICINE RIGHT INTO A VEIN.

VEINS ARE BLOOD VESSELS THAT CARRY BLOOD TOWARD YOUR HEART.

CHEMO GIVEN THROUGH THE BLOODSTREAM IS CALLED *IV* OR INTRAVENOUS CHEMO.

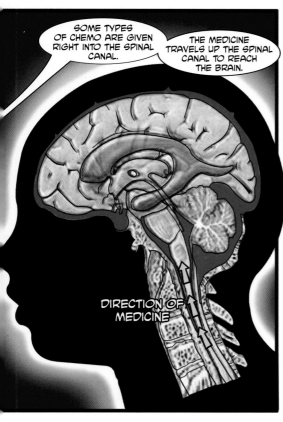

SOME TYPES OF CHEMO ARE GIVEN RIGHT INTO THE SPINAL CANAL.

THE MEDICINE TRAVELS UP THE SPINAL CANAL TO REACH THE BRAIN.

DIRECTION OF MEDICINE

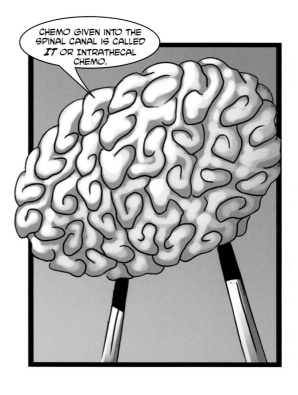

CHEMO GIVEN INTO THE SPINAL CANAL IS CALLED *IT* OR INTRATHECAL CHEMO.

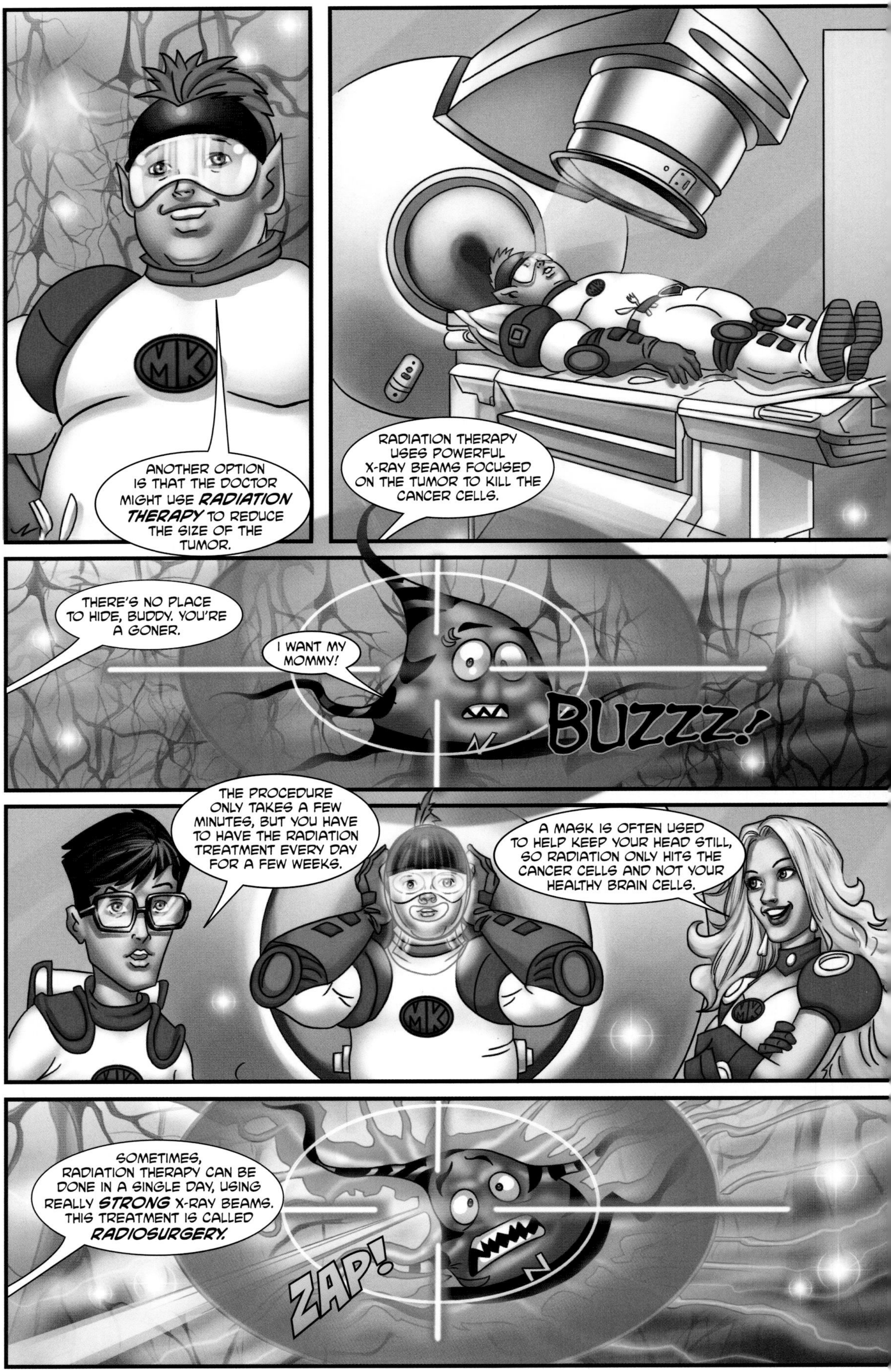
ANOTHER OPTION IS THAT THE DOCTOR MIGHT USE RADIATION THERAPY TO REDUCE THE SIZE OF THE TUMOR.
RADIATION THERAPY USES POWERFUL X-RAY BEAMS FOCUSED ON THE TUMOR TO KILL THE CANCER CELLS.
THERE'S NO PLACE TO HIDE, BUDDY. YOU'RE A GONER.
I WANT MY MOMMY!
BUZZZ!
THE PROCEDURE ONLY TAKES A FEW MINUTES, BUT YOU HAVE TO HAVE THE RADIATION TREATMENT EVERY DAY FOR A FEW WEEKS.
A MASK IS OFTEN USED TO HELP KEEP YOUR HEAD STILL, SO RADIATION ONLY HITS THE CANCER CELLS AND NOT YOUR HEALTHY BRAIN CELLS.
SOMETIMES, RADIATION THERAPY CAN BE DONE IN A SINGLE DAY, USING REALLY STRONG X-RAY BEAMS. THIS TREATMENT IS CALLED RADIOSURGERY.
ZAP!

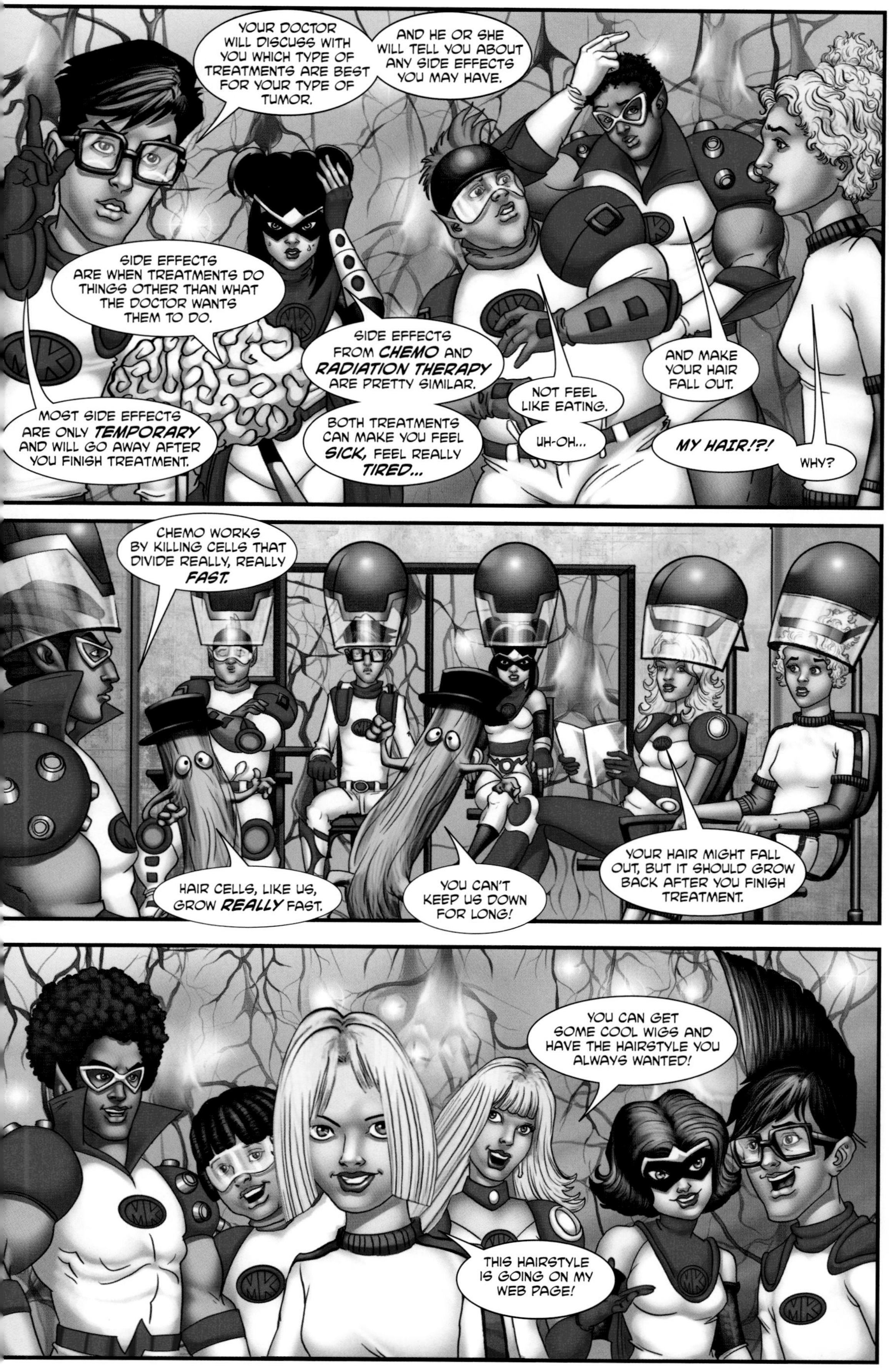
YOUR DOCTOR WILL DISCUSS WITH YOU WHICH TYPE OF TREATMENTS ARE BEST FOR YOUR TYPE OF TUMOR.
AND HE OR SHE WILL TELL YOU ABOUT ANY SIDE EFFECTS YOU MAY HAVE.
SIDE EFFECTS ARE WHEN TREATMENTS DO THINGS OTHER THAN WHAT THE DOCTOR WANTS THEM TO DO.
MOST SIDE EFFECTS ARE ONLY TEMPORARY AND WILL GO AWAY AFTER YOU FINISH TREATMENT.
SIDE EFFECTS FROM CHEMO AND RADIATION THERAPY ARE PRETTY SIMILAR.
BOTH TREATMENTS CAN MAKE YOU FEEL SICK, FEEL REALLY TIRED...
NOT FEEL LIKE EATING.
UH-OH...
AND MAKE YOUR HAIR FALL OUT.
MY HAIR!?!
WHY?
CHEMO WORKS BY KILLING CELLS THAT DIVIDE REALLY, REALLY FAST.
HAIR CELLS, LIKE US, GROW REALLY FAST.
YOU CAN'T KEEP US DOWN FOR LONG!
YOUR HAIR MIGHT FALL OUT, BUT IT SHOULD GROW BACK AFTER YOU FINISH TREATMENT.
YOU CAN GET SOME COOL WIGS AND HAVE THE HAIRSTYLE YOU ALWAYS WANTED!
THIS HAIRSTYLE IS GOING ON MY WEB PAGE!

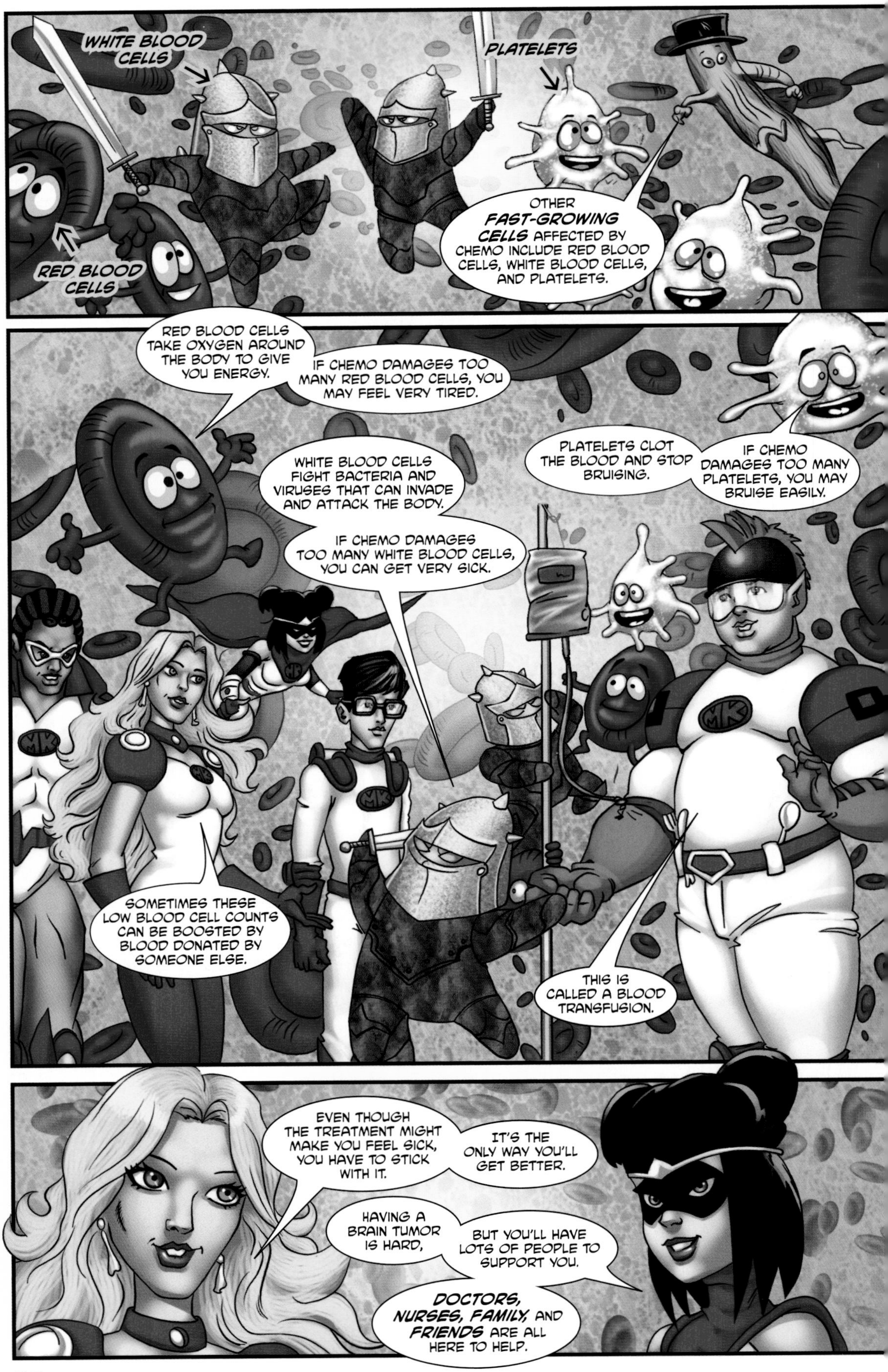
WHITE BLOOD CELLS
PLATELETS
RED BLOOD CELLS
OTHER FAST-GROWING CELLS AFFECTED BY CHEMO INCLUDE RED BLOOD CELLS, WHITE BLOOD CELLS, AND PLATELETS.
RED BLOOD CELLS TAKE OXYGEN AROUND THE BODY TO GIVE YOU ENERGY.
IF CHEMO DAMAGES TOO MANY RED BLOOD CELLS, YOU MAY FEEL VERY TIRED.
WHITE BLOOD CELLS FIGHT BACTERIA AND VIRUSES THAT CAN INVADE AND ATTACK THE BODY.
IF CHEMO DAMAGES TOO MANY WHITE BLOOD CELLS, YOU CAN GET VERY SICK.
PLATELETS CLOT THE BLOOD AND STOP BRUISING.
IF CHEMO DAMAGES TOO MANY PLATELETS, YOU MAY BRUISE EASILY.
SOMETIMES THESE LOW BLOOD CELL COUNTS CAN BE BOOSTED BY BLOOD DONATED BY SOMEONE ELSE.
THIS IS CALLED A BLOOD TRANSFUSION.
EVEN THOUGH THE TREATMENT MIGHT MAKE YOU FEEL SICK, YOU HAVE TO STICK WITH IT.
IT'S THE ONLY WAY YOU'LL GET BETTER.
HAVING A BRAIN TUMOR IS HARD,
BUT YOU'LL HAVE LOTS OF PEOPLE TO SUPPORT YOU.
DOCTORS, NURSES, FAMILY, AND FRIENDS ARE ALL HERE TO HELP.

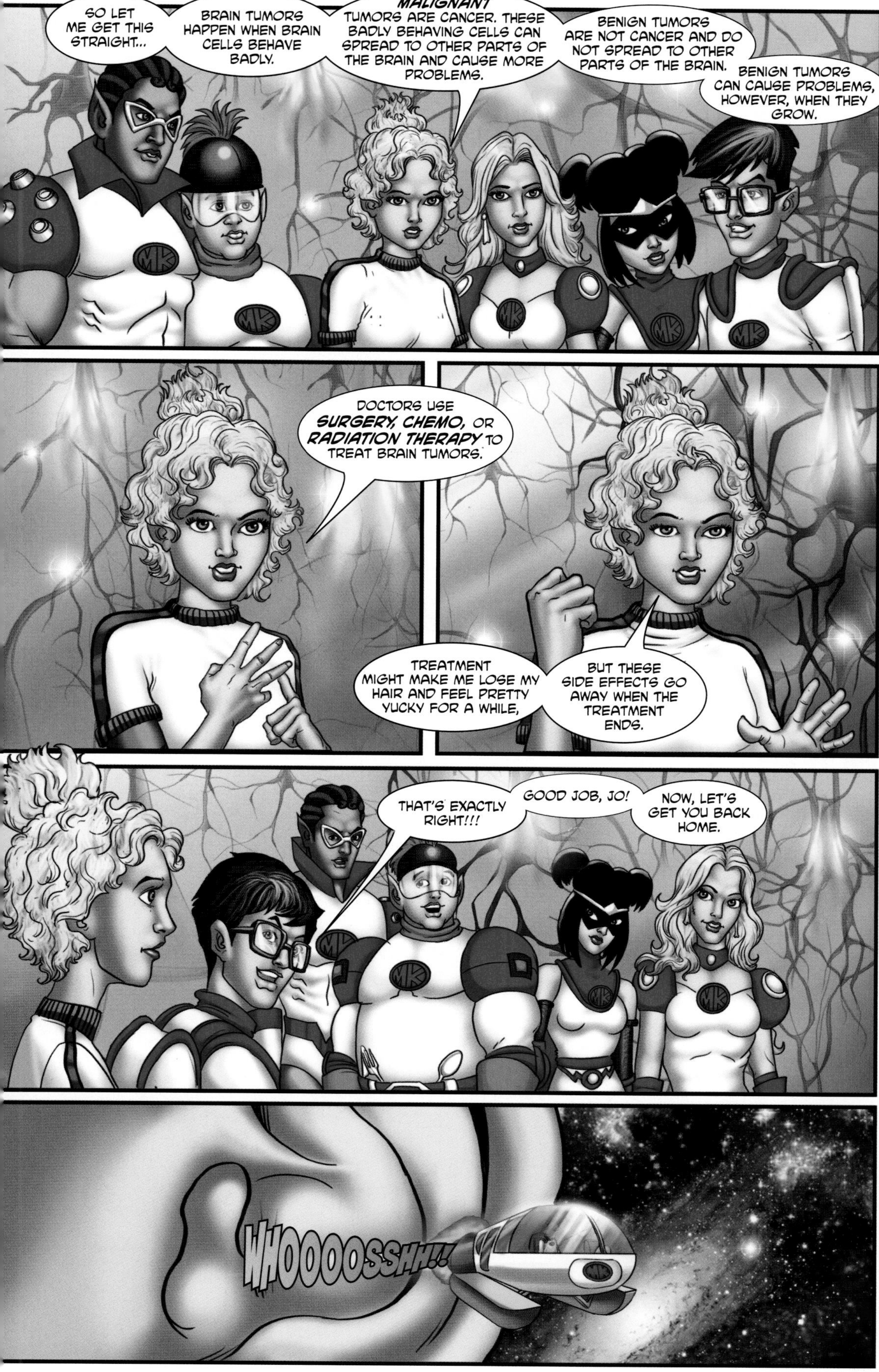
SO LET ME GET THIS STRAIGHT...
BRAIN TUMORS HAPPEN WHEN BRAIN CELLS BEHAVE BADLY.
MALIGNANT TUMORS ARE CANCER. THESE BADLY BEHAVING CELLS CAN SPREAD TO OTHER PARTS OF THE BRAIN AND CAUSE MORE PROBLEMS.
BENIGN TUMORS ARE NOT CANCER AND DO NOT SPREAD TO OTHER PARTS OF THE BRAIN.
BENIGN TUMORS CAN CAUSE PROBLEMS, HOWEVER, WHEN THEY GROW.
DOCTORS USE SURGERY, CHEMO, OR RADIATION THERAPY TO TREAT BRAIN TUMORS.
TREATMENT MIGHT MAKE ME LOSE MY HAIR AND FEEL PRETTY YUCKY FOR A WHILE,
BUT THESE SIDE EFFECTS GO AWAY WHEN THE TREATMENT ENDS.
THAT'S EXACTLY RIGHT!!!
GOOD JOB, JO!
NOW, LET'S GET YOU BACK HOME.
WHOOOOSSHH!!

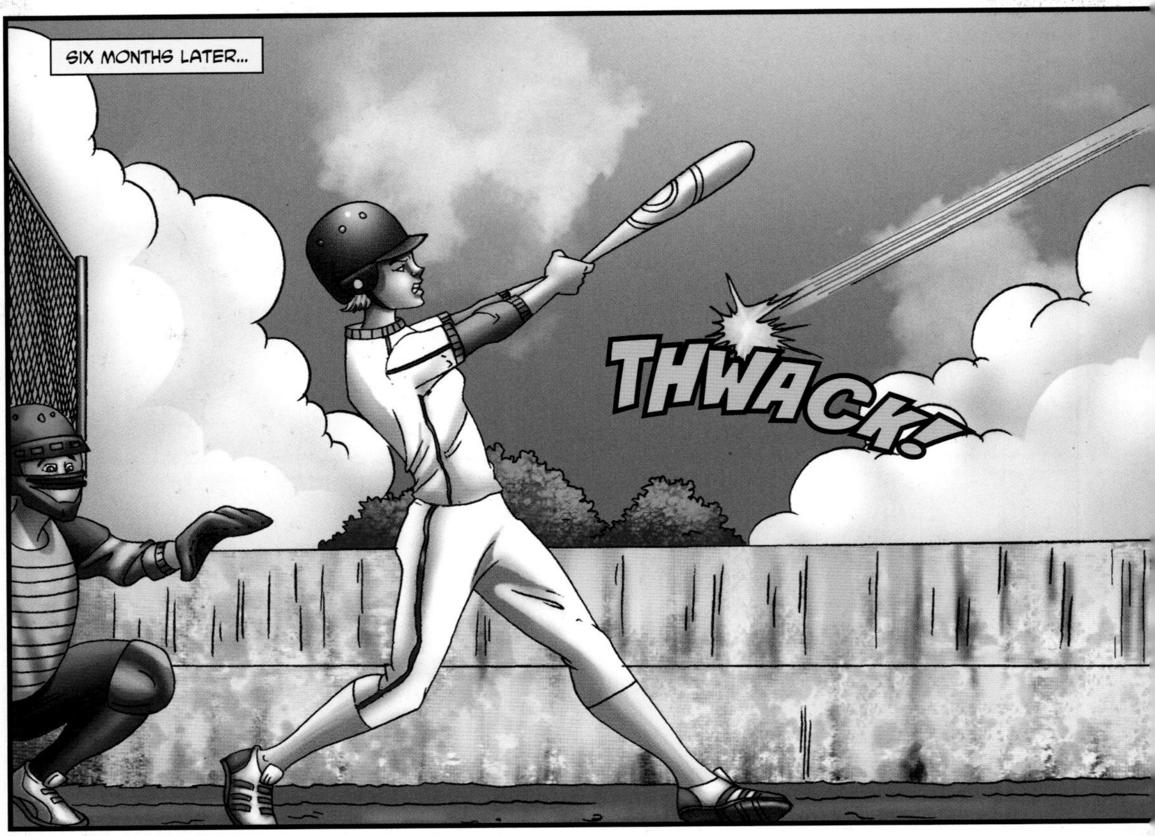
SIX MONTHS LATER...
THWACK!

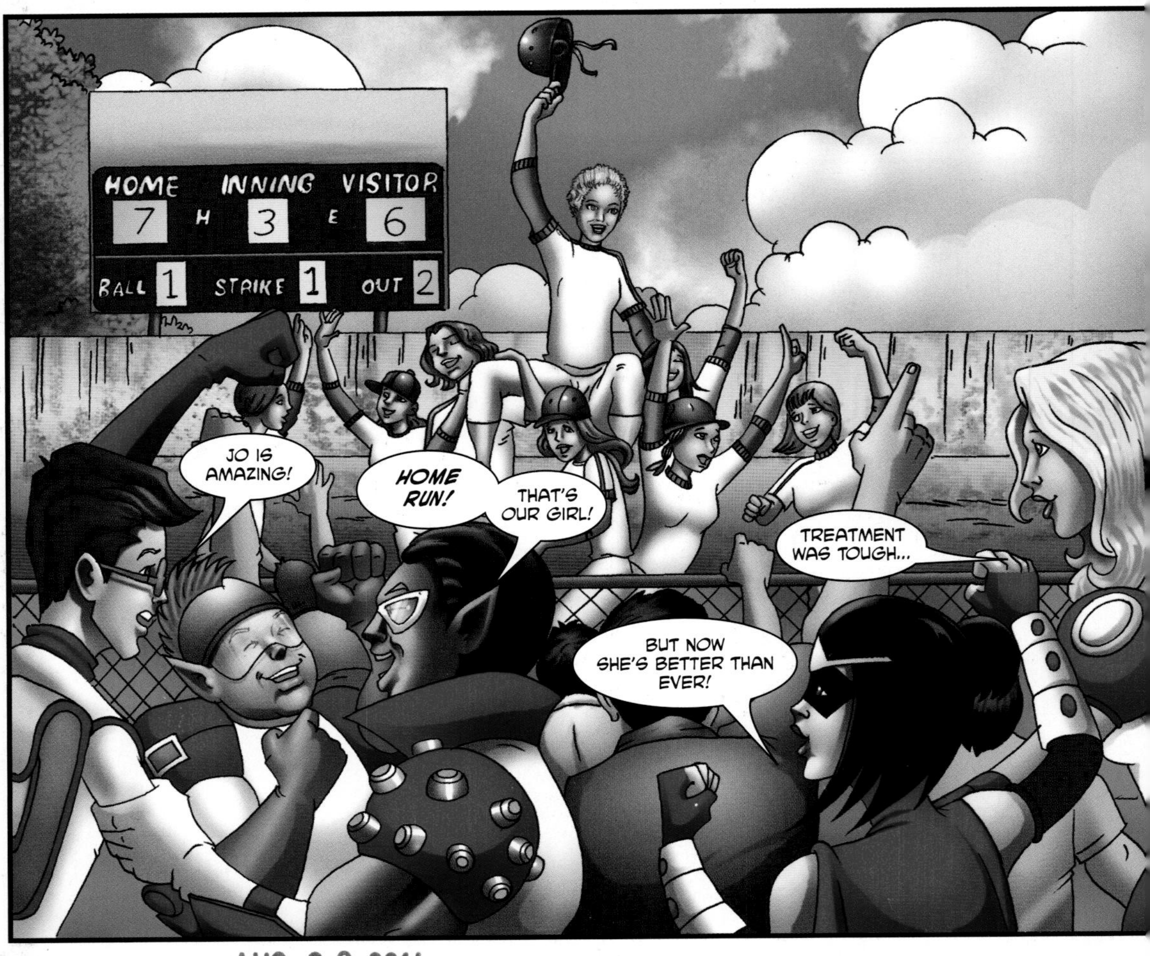
HOME INNING VISITOR
7 H 3 E 6
BALL 1 STRIKE 1 OUT 2
JO IS AMAZING!
HOME RUN!
THAT'S OUR GIRL!
TREATMENT WAS TOUGH...
BUT NOW SHE'S BETTER THAN EVER!